LIVING STREAM MINISTRY

The ALL-INCLUSIVE CHRIST

WITNESS LEE

Anaheim, California • www.lsm.org

First Edition, 1969.

ISBN 0-87083-020-1

Published by

Living Stream Ministry
2431 W. La Palma Ave., Anaheim, CA 92801 U.S.A.
P. O. Box 2121, Anaheim, CA 92814 U.S.A.

Printed in the United States of America

06 07 08 09 10 11 / 18 17 16 15 14 13 12

CONTENTS

PREFACE

This book is composed of messages given by Brother Witness Lee in December 1962 in Los Angeles, California.

CHAPTER ONE

THE ALL-INCLUSIVE CHRIST— AN INTRODUCTION

Scripture Reading: Gen. 1:1, 2, 9-12, 26, 27, 29; 7:17; 8:1, 13, 22; 12:1, 7; Exo. 3:8; 6:8; Ezek. 20:40-42; 1 Cor. 1:30; Col. 2:6, 7, 16, 17; 3:11; Eph. 2:12; Gal. 5:4

In this series of messages we want to see something of the land of Canaan, which is the type of the all-inclusive Christ. We also want to see how the city and the temple, which were built on this land of Canaan, are types of the fullness of Christ, which is His Body, the church. Thus, what we will consider is the all-inclusive Christ, out of which and upon which the fullness of Christ, the church, is built. Remember well that it is not just Christ and the church but the all-inclusive Christ and the fullness of Christ which is His Body, the church.

CHRIST THE REALITY OF ALL

First of all, I would ask you to realize that according to the Scriptures all physical things, all the material things that we see, touch, and enjoy, are not the real things. They are but a shadow, a figure of the true. Day by day we are contacting so many material objects: we are eating food, drinking water, putting on clothes; we are living in our houses and driving in our cars. I would ask you to realize and remember well that all these things are not real. They are but shadows, figures. The food we take every day is not the real food but a figure of the real. The water we drink is not the real water. The light before our eyes is not the real light but a figure pointing to something else.

Then what are the real things? Brothers and sisters, I would by the grace of God tell you in truth that the real things are nothing but Christ Himself. Christ is the real food to us. Christ is the real water to us. Christ is the real light to us. Christ is the reality of everything to us. Even our physical life is not a real life. It is but a figure pointing to Christ. Christ is the real life to us. If you don't have Christ, you don't have life. You will say, "I am living; I have life in my body!" But you must realize that this is not the real life. It is merely a shadow pointing to the real life which is Christ Himself.

Day by day while living in my house, I have the realization and feeling that it is not my real dwelling. One day I said to the Lord, "Lord, this is not my dwelling place; this is not the real one; this is nothing. Lord, You Yourself are my dwelling place." Yes, He is the real habitation to us.

Now I would ask you a question. Probably this has never occurred to you. You may be quite clear that Christ is your food, that Christ is your living water, that Christ is your light, and that Christ is your life. But let me ask you, have you ever realized that Christ is the very land on which you are living? Christ is the land. You may feel that day by day you are living on this earth, on this piece of land, but you must realize that this earth is not your real land. Even this earth is nothing but a figure pointing to Christ. Christ is the real land to us. Food is a figure, water is a figure, light is a figure, our life is a figure, and the land is a figure too. Christ is the real land to us. I must tell you that I have been a Christian for more than thirty years, but never until recent years did I have the thought that Christ is the land to me. I knew that Christ to me is the life, the light, the food and everything, but not the land.

In the last few years the Lord has brought me to experience Him more and more. Before the Lord showed me that He is the land to us, He first showed me that He is our dwelling place. I had read the Scriptures day by day for more than twenty years without noticing that the Lord is our dwelling place. Then one day I saw something from the ninetieth Psalm. In the first verse Moses said, "Lord, You are our dwelling place from generation to generation." Oh, that day the Lord opened my eyes to see that He is my dwelling place. At that time I knew the Lord as something more. But after two or three years the Lord opened my eyes even further. I saw that the Lord is not only the dwelling place to me, but also the land. The Lord is the land to me! Oh, from that time the Lord has shown me many things from the Scriptures. From that time I began to understand why in the Old Testament the Lord always referred to a piece of land. The Lord called out Abraham, telling him that He would bring him to a certain land, which was the land of Canaan. You can recall how many times from the twelfth chapter of Genesis to the end of the Old Testament the Lord stressed and referred to the land again and again. The land...the land...the land I promised to thy fathers. The land I promised Abraham; the land I promised Isaac; the land I promised Jacob; the land I promised you. I will bring you into the land. It was the land, the land, always the land.

THE CENTER OF GOD'S ETERNAL PLAN

The center of the Old Testament is the temple within the city. This temple within the city was built on that piece of land, and this piece of land with the temple and the city built upon it is the very center of the Old Testament Scriptures. It is also the very center of God's mind. In God's mind is this piece of land with its temple and city.

If we know the Scriptures and have light from God, we will realize that the center of God's eternal plan, typically speaking, is the land with its temple and the city. The Old Testament, from the first chapter of Genesis, always takes the land as the center, always mentions something related to the land.

Let us look at the first chapter of Genesis. Perhaps you are so familiar with that chapter that you could even recite it. But one thing may be hidden from you. In the first chapter of Genesis there is something very important hidden beneath the surface. It is *the land*. Please consider. What is the purpose and aim of God's creation according to the record of the first chapter of Genesis? It is nothing but the recovery of the land. God wanted to recover the land and do something upon it. "In the beginning God created the heavens *and the earth*." What about the earth? There was chaos upon the earth. Waste and void and deep waters were upon it. It was buried under the deep. So God came in to work; God began to recover the earth. He divided the light from the darkness and the waters which were above from the waters which were beneath. Then He divided the water from the earth, and the earth came out from the waters on the third day. It was the third day when the Lord Jesus Christ came out of the depths of death. So, you see, this is a type. On the third day God brought the earth out of the waters of death. From this type you can realize what the earth is. The earth, or the land, is a type of Christ.

Then after the land came out of the waters, what happened? Oh, all kinds of life came into being—grass, herbs producing seed, and fruit trees yielding fruit. I think that now you see the picture. After the resurrection of Christ, after the Lord was brought out of death, He produced abundant life. Yes, He was full of the production of life. Then on this land which was full of life, man was created according to the image of God, having the likeness of God, and to this man was committed God's authority. After the Lord came out of death, there was an abundance of life produced, and in the midst of this fullness of life a man was created who was the representative of God, with God's image, God's likeness, and God's authority. All these things have transpired in Christ as a piece of land.

Now you know what is meant by the land. The land is but a figure of Christ as everything to us. Everything that God prepared for mankind is concentrated in the land. Man was created to live on the land to enjoy all the provision of God. All things related to man are concentrated in the land, which is a type of Christ. All things which God has prepared for us are concentrated in Christ.

Later you will see how God brought His people into the promised land and how His people remained there and enjoyed all its riches. The result was that the city and the temple came into being. The city and the temple are the result of the enjoyment of this land. What is the city and the temple? The city is the center of God's authority, God's kingdom, and the temple is the center of God's house, God's dwelling place. The kingdom of God and the house of God are the result of the enjoyment of the land. When the people of God enjoy this land to a certain extent, something comes into existence—the authority of God and the presence of God, or, in other words, the kingdom of God and the house of God. If we possess Christ as a piece of land and enjoy all His riches, after a certain extent something will issue forth—the church with God's kingdom, the temple in the city.

Now you can apply all these things to the Old Testament and New Testament Scriptures. In principle, everything recorded in the Old Testament is exactly the same as that in the New; there is no difference. God's intention revealed in both the Old and New Testaments is that Christ should be the land to us. We have the ground to enjoy all the riches of Christ. God gave us this ground. After a certain amount of enjoyment of His riches, something will issue forth—the kingdom of God and the house of God, the church with God's kingdom. This is the central thought of God's eternal plan.

THE BATTLE FOR THE LAND

If you read the Scriptures carefully, you will see a very grim and serious activity being carried on. Satan, the enemy of God, has done his utmost and is still doing his utmost to frustrate the people of God from enjoying this piece of land. He will do whatever he can to spoil the enjoyment of Christ as the land. Read the Scriptures. Not long after God created the heavens and the earth with the intention of giving the earth to mankind as an enjoyment, Satan did something to frustrate Him. Because of Satan's rebellion, God had to judge the universe, and due to that judgment the earth was buried beneath the waters of the deep. This hindered God's plan for some time. Then God came in to work and do something, and as we have seen already, He recovered the land from the waters of the deep. Upon this recovered land, an abundance of life came into being. And then a life with the image of God and committed with the authority of God came forth. However, we know that it was not long after this before the enemy came in again. He deceived man and put God in a position where judgment upon the earth was again imperative. The recovered earth was once more put under the waters of the deep: the flood came and covered the whole earth, and typically speaking man was separated from the enjoyment of the land which is Christ. Remember the phrase in Ephesians, *apart from Christ* (2:12)? All those people who were under the judgment of the flood were a type of people separated from Christ. To be separated from the earth, figuratively speaking, is to be separated from Christ. But through the redemption of the ark, Noah and his family obtained the right to possess the land and enjoy all its riches. The ark brought them back to the enjoyment of the land. The flood separated people from the earth, but the ark brought people back to the earth. Once more man took possession of the land and enjoyed its riches. But again, it was not long before the enemy did something more to spoil the enjoyment of the earth. So, out of that race made rebellious by Satan, God called one man, Abraham, and told him that He would bring him to a certain land. Now you realize that God's work is always to recover the land. The enemy's work is always to frustrate, to spoil, to hinder, to do something to put the land in chaos. Now the Lord once more brought His chosen one to the land. But then, you remember well, it was not long before even this chosen one gradually drifted away from the land into Egypt. Yes, and the Lord brought him back once more to this piece of land. And then his sons, the people of Israel all left this land and went down into Egypt. Then, after a long period, the Lord once more brought all the people up from Egypt and back to this very piece of land. Again, after a period of time, the enemy moved again and sent the Chaldeans, the army from Babylon, to spoil the land and capture the people from it. And again, after seventy years, the Lord brought them back once more to this piece of land.

I tell you, this is the history of the Old Testament. How many times did the Lord recover this land? At least five or six times. The Lord created it, but the enemy spoiled it. The Lord came in to recover, but the enemy countered with something else. The Lord moved again to recover, but the enemy again reacted. Oh, here is the struggle! Do you see? Here is the battle!

I would ask you to consider the purpose of these battles recorded in the Old Testament. For what purpose were they fought? You must see that they were all focused upon the land.

The enemy came to assault the land, to take over the land. Then God moved to fight for His people and recover the land. All the battles in the Old Testament were concerned with this piece of land.

THE MEASURE OF OUR EXPERIENCE OF CHRIST

What is this piece of land? Never forget, this land is the all-inclusive Christ. Not just Christ, but the all-inclusive Christ. If I were to ask you if you have Christ, you would answer, "Oh, praise the Lord, I have Him; I have Christ!" But I would ask you what kind of Christ you have. I am afraid that in your experience you have just a little Christ, a poor Christ, not an all-inclusive Christ.

Let me tell you a story, a real story. Not long after I was saved, I studied the Scriptures, and I was taught that the passover lamb was the type of Christ. Oh, when I learned this, how I praised the Lord! I exclaimed, "Lord, I praise You, You are the lamb; You are the lamb for me!" But I would ask you to compare the lamb with the land. What kind of comparison can you make between a little lamb and a great land? What is the lamb? You must say that it is Christ. But I would tell you that it is a little Christ. That was not the goal of God for His people. God never told them, "All right, as long as you have the lamb, that is sufficient." No. God told them in effect that the reason He gave them the lamb was to bring them into the land. The passover was *for the land.*

Do you have Christ? Yes, you have Christ. But what kind of Christ do you have, a lamb or a land? All the people of Israel had the lamb on that Passover Day in Egypt, but very few, I'm sorry to say, got into the land. Very few took possession of that piece of land.

After I was saved for one or two years, I was taught that the manna which the children of Israel enjoyed in the wilderness was also a type of Christ. I was so joyful. I said, "Lord, You are my food; You are not only the lamb to me, but also my daily manna." But, I would ask you, is the manna the purpose, the goal of God? Did God deliver His people from Egypt to enjoy the manna in the wilderness? No! The land is the purpose; the land is the goal. Do you enjoy Christ as the land? I doubt it, and I venture to say that even you doubt it. You can say that you enjoy the lamb as your passover and the Lord as your daily manna, but very few can really say that they enjoy the all-inclusive Christ as the land.

The Word tells us in Colossians 2 that we have been rooted in Christ. Now I would ask you to consider: If we have been rooted in Christ, then what is Christ to us? Yes, Christ is the earth; Christ is the soil. A plant or a tree is rooted in the soil, in the land. Even so, we have been rooted in Christ. I am afraid you have never realized that Christ is the very soil, the very land to you. You are a little plant rooted in this land which is Christ Himself. I must confess that five or six years ago, I never had such a thought. I read the Scriptures and spent much time in the book of Colossians. I read it over and over, but never obtained this light. I never knew that Christ is the soil, my very earth. It was not until the last few years that my eyes were opened.

I deeply feel that most of the Lord's children are still remaining in Egypt. They have only experienced the passover; they have just taken the Lord as the lamb. They have been saved by the lamb, but they have not been delivered out of this world. Yes, some have come out of Egypt, some have been delivered from the world, but they are still wandering in the wilderness. They enjoy Christ a little more; they enjoy Him as their daily manna. They can boast that they enjoy Christ as their food and they are so satisfied. But, brothers and sisters, is this good enough? I think when we meet those who enjoy Christ as their daily manna, we are very happy. We say, "Oh, praise the Lord, here are some brothers and sisters who really enjoy the Lord as their manna day by day!" But we must realize that this falls far short of God's purpose. God's purpose is not just that we enjoy Christ a little, but that He should be the all-inclusive One to us. Look at this verse: "As therefore you have received the Christ, Jesus the Lord, walk in Him" (Col. 2:6). He is a sphere, a realm for us to walk in. He is not just some food or water, but a realm, a land within which we can walk. We must walk in Him. He is our land, He is our earth, He is our kingdom. Walk in Him.

I believe that the picture is very clear. In Egypt was the lamb, in the wilderness was the manna, and ahead of the people of Israel was the land of Canaan. That is the goal; that land is the goal of God. We have to enter in. It is our portion. It is the all-inclusive gift of God to us. We must take possession of it. It is ours, but we must enjoy it.

In these days we have been speaking much about the church and the expression of the Body of Christ. But you and I must realize that if we are not able to take possession of Christ as the all-inclusive One and experience Him, there can never be the reality of the church. You and I must realize that we have been rooted in Christ as a plant rooted in the soil. We must possess Christ as everything to us, not just in words or in doctrine but in practical reality. We must realize that just as the soil is everything to that plant, so Christ is everything to us. We must realize this to such an extent that we can experience Christ. You and I have already been rooted, but we do not realize the fact, we do not take possession of the fact. Colossians tells us that having been rooted, we are being built up in Him with others. If we have no experience of having been rooted in Christ, how can we be built up with others? That is why the building up of the church among the Lord's people is almost nil. How could there be a temple and a city when the people of Israel were still wandering in the wilderness? Since they were not in possession of the land, it was impossible. How can there be the real building up of the church? How can there be the real expression of the Body of Christ? It can only be by realizing and experiencing Christ as everything to us. Brothers and sisters, may the Lord open our eyes.

SOME PRACTICAL EXAMPLES

Day by day we are speaking many words. But do you realize that all our words must be Christ? Do you speak Christ? Do you take Christ as your words? If you do not, you are speaking nonsense. Perhaps you will ask what I mean. I mean this: if you have received light to see that in God's mind Christ is everything, the Holy Spirit will lead you to the place where you realize that even the words you speak day by day must be Christ. You will accept the work of the cross upon your mouth and upon your words. You will be renewed in your speaking. You will be renewed in your language. You will experience Christ to such an extent that you will say, "Lord, if what I am going to say is not of You, I will not say it. I apply the cross to my mouth. I apply the cross to my speaking so that I may be renewed by You in my words."

Let me give you a few more examples of how we must realize Christ as everything to us. Whenever we are going to eat, we should immediately have the registration within us that Christ is our real food. We have to say, "Lord, this is not my true food; You are the food by which I live. Man does not really live by this food, but by Yourself. Lord, I would spend more time taking You than eating this food." When we are going to rest, we must say, "Lord, You are my rest; You are my true rest!" Whatever we are going to do, whatever we are going to enjoy and experience, we must realize that Christ is that very thing.

Sisters, you are the ones who are always doing the shopping. Have you ever thought that Christ is that very thing for which you are going to shop? I believe very few of you have had such a thought. Perhaps you have heard a message about Christ being everything to us; you have sung Hallelujah in the meeting, but immediately afterward you have forgotten everything. If you have received true light from the Lord, the Holy Spirit will point out Christ to you in a practical way day by day, step by step. He will show you that whatever you are going to buy must be a figure of Christ. You will not want to pay the price for anything outside of Christ. You will say, "I wish to gain Christ; I want to have more of Christ." You can apply Christ to everything.

Young people, when you are going to study, you can say, "Lord, You are my book. I would read You; I would study You much more than these books. I would apply You at this very moment while I am reading."

Try to exercise in such a way day by day. Take Christ as the land; take Him as everything to you—not just as food, not just as the light, not just as your dwelling place, but as the all-inclusive land. You must realize that Christ is the all-inclusive One to you. You must practice to experience Christ and apply Him in everything. Then, I believe something will issue forth from you, and that something will be the building of the church in God's kingdom, the temple in the city. This is the purpose of God.

CHAPTER TWO

THE GOODNESS OF THE LAND—
ITS SPACIOUSNESS

Scripture Reading: Deut. 12:9; Heb. 4:8, 9, 11; Eph. 3:17, 18;
Phil. 3:7, 8, 10, 12-14; Exo. 3:8; Deut. 4:25

We have seen in the Old Testament that the land with its
temple and city is the center of God's plan. What God planned
to do on this earth was to obtain that piece of land with the
temple and the city built upon it. The temple is the center of
God's presence, and the city is the center of God's authority.
God's presence and God's authority could only be realized by
the temple and the city built upon that piece of land. I must
ask you to consider the whole record of the Old Testament
more and more. The entire Old Testament deals with that
piece of land and its temple and city.

THE ALL-INCLUSIVE TYPE OF CHRIST

We have already seen that this land is the full type, the all-
inclusive type of Christ. We know that there are many types
in the Old Testament. We know that the passover lamb is a
type of Christ, and we know that the manna is a type of Christ.
The tabernacle with all its furniture, utensils, and various
offerings is also a type of Christ. But I wish to point out to you
that without this piece of land, there is no all-inclusive type of
Christ. The passover lamb is not the all-inclusive type, and
neither is the manna or even the tabernacle with all the
things related to it. Many different kinds of offerings were
ordained by the Lord, but they only depicted various aspects
of Christ. Only the land of Canaan is the full type, the
all-inclusive type of Christ. We have all accepted Christ as
our Redeemer. That is quite wonderful! But we must realize

that Christ as the Redeemer is not the all-inclusive One. We
are told in the Scriptures that Christ is all and in all, that
Christ is the all-inclusive One. Everything is in Him and He
is in everything. There is no other type in the Old Testament
but the land of Canaan which shows Him as such.

What do we mean by the word *all-inclusive?* We are told
that Christ is the light, but this is not all-inclusive. We are
told that Christ is our life, but this also is not all-inclusive.
We are told that Christ is the food and the living water, but
even these do not make Him the all-inclusive One. Christ is
all and in all. Christ is not only the light, the life, the food,
and the living water, but Christ is everything to us. Whatever
you need, whatever you contact, whatever you obtain, whatever you enjoy, whatever you experience—all these things must
be Christ. Christ is the all-inclusive One to us.

We are not speaking doctrinally but very practically. Whenever you do something, whenever you enjoy something,
whenever you use something, you must immediately apply
Christ. For instance, you are sitting on a seat. Do you realize
that this is not the real seat? This is but a shadow, a figure
pointing to Christ. Christ is the real seat. If you do not have
Christ, it means that in your entire life you have never had a
seat. There is no rest for you. You have nothing to rely upon.
You have something false, for Christ is the real thing.

Let me tell you something which may sound strange to
you. Sometimes when I put on my glasses, I say, "Lord, these
are not real glasses; You are my real glasses. Without You, I
can see nothing. Without You, I have no sight." Christ is
everything to us. If you have Christ and the way to experience
Him, you have everything. If you do not have Christ and know
not how to apply Him and experience Him in such a practical
way, you have nothing.

When you are climbing the stairs, do you realize that
Christ is the real stairs to you? You are told that Christ is the
way, and without Him there is no way. So when you are walking or driving, you must say, "Lord, You are my way. Without
You I have no way, I have no way to do things, I have no way to
go on, I have no way to be a person." Christ is everything to
us, so Christ is our way.

Many times during the past years of serving the Lord I have encountered problems between the husband and wife. Many times the brothers have come to me and said, "Brother Lee, would you kindly tell me a better way to deal with my wife?" My answer is always this: "Brother, there is no 'better way.' The better way is Christ Himself. And I would say the best way is Christ Himself." Almost every time I answer in such a way, people do not understand. They always query, "What do you mean by that?" So I tell them, "Brother, I mean that Christ is the best way for you to deal with your dear wife." Sometimes they press me to tell them in detail how to live, how to get along, and how to deal with their wives. Then I tell them, "Brother, I have told you clearly, Christ is the best way for you to deal with your wife. It's quite simple. Forget about everything. Just come to the Lord in your spirit to have a personal contact with Him. Come and tell Him, 'Lord, You are my life, You are my way, You are everything to me. So I come to You once more to take You as everything. I take You as the way to deal with my wife.' Then be assured that you will know. I cannot tell you what to do, but the Lord Himself will be your way. Believe me."

The sisters especially like to go into detail about their marital problems. They say, "Oh, brother, please give me some time. Be patient with me. Let me tell you the whole story." I tell them, "Sister, I have the patience; I am ready to listen to you. But I tell you, it is all useless. The more you say, the more you tell me about this and that, the more you will get into trouble. Be simple. Just kneel down and from your spirit say something to the Lord. Don't say something to me. This doesn't mean I don't want to hear you, but I cannot point out any better way than Christ Himself. You have to contact Christ once more." Eventually most of the brothers and sisters have been convinced and have come to know something of Christ in a practical way. They have come to me and said, "Now I know that Christ is the best way for me to deal with my wife"; "Christ is the best way for me to deal with my husband."

You see, this is not merely a doctrine or some sort of teaching. You must experience it. You must apply Christ to your daily life.

The people of Israel enjoyed the passover lamb and then the manna day by day for forty years, but they were never fully satisfied. They just applied a little of Christ; they just experienced a small portion of Christ. Not until they entered the land of Canaan was He everything to them and were they fully satisfied. When they entered the land, what they ate came from the land, what they drank came from the land—all their living came out of the land. The land was everything to them. No other type in the Old Testament is so all-inclusive as the land of Canaan.

THE REST FOR THE PEOPLE OF GOD

We must realize why God said that this land was the rest for His people. The lamb was not the rest. The manna was not the rest. But the land is the rest. The people of Israel enjoyed the passover lamb, but they did not enter into rest. They enjoyed the manna day by day for forty years, but they still did not enter into rest. We know what rest is. Rest is something complete, something in full, something perfect. When you have everything, then you can really rest. Since the passover lamb was not the complete and perfect portion for God's people, it was not the rest. It was good to a certain point, but it was not the rest. The manna too was good in a particular aspect, but it was not the full, the perfect, and the complete portion. Only the land was the rest to the people of God, because the land was the completion, the perfection, and the fullness. In the land you have everything; the land will satisfy you.

By Hebrews 3 and 4, we may realize that the land which was the rest to the people of Israel is the type of Christ. Christ is the rest because Christ is everything to us. Most of us are still not in the position to realize Christ as the all-inclusive One. We just know Him as our Savior, as our Redeemer, as our life, and as our way. Very few of us know Christ as everything to us. The land is the goal; the land is the aim; the land is the eternal purpose of God. Unless we are able to realize Christ as the land, we are lacking. We must see that there is much more than what we have experienced of Christ. We have only a little experience of Him. This is what burdens us very much in these days. We do believe the Lord is going to recover this.

THE GOODNESS OF THE LAND

Many times in the Old Testament this piece of land is called *a good land.* It is really remarkable. "I will bring you into *a good land.*" If you do not pay special attention to this, you will feel that it is just an ordinary statement. We are always saying that something is good; it becomes just an ordinary mode of description to us with no special significance attached to it. But when the Lord says that something is good, we must pay attention. This is not commonplace. And He says it over and over: a good land...a good land...a good land! It must really be good!

What is the goodness of this land? Since the Lord said that it is a good land, what then is its goodness? In the past most of us have not paid much attention to this matter. We have just taken it as the good land and let it go at that, not inquiring into the reason for its goodness.

It is rather difficult to fully define the goodness of this land. First of all, I will point out to you a rather peculiar definition. You have read it already. Exodus 3:8 says, "I am come... to bring them up out of that land unto a good land and a large" (ASV)—a large land. Mr. J. N. Darby informs us that it is better to translate the word *large* as "spacious." It is a good and spacious land. It is good first of all in *spaciousness.*

You understand what spaciousness is. But can you describe the spaciousness of this land? Can you tell us the extent, the expanse, of Christ? In other words, do you know how big Christ is? Every one of us has a certain measurement, but what is the measurement of Christ? The apostle Paul gives it to us in Ephesians 3. The measurements of Christ are *the breadth, the length, the height, and the depth.* Can you tell how broad is the breadth, how long is the length, how high is the height, and how deep is the depth? If you asked me, I would have to say, "I don't know. It is unlimited." The breadth of Christ is the breadth of the universe. Christ is the breadth, Christ is the length, Christ is the height, and Christ is the depth of the whole universe. If the universe has a limit, that limit must be Christ. You can never measure the dimensions of Christ. This is the first item of the goodness of the land. The land is good in the unlimited measurement of Christ.

APPLYING THE SPACIOUSNESS OF CHRIST

Now I would ask you, How can you apply this? Can you apply the measurement of Christ? Can you apply the breadth, the length, the height, and the depth? Let me illustrate. One day a sister came to me and said, "Brother, you know my family. You know that my husband is such and such a person." "Yes," I said, "I know, I know." "And you know I have five children, and one more is coming—that will make six. I am still young, and I am afraid that after the sixth there may be more. Brother, I am concerned about this situation." Then I asked her, "Sister, do you know how big Christ is?" She said, "Oh, brother, this is a strange question. I have never thought about that. What do you mean?" Then I brought her to realize that the Christ whom she had received is an unlimited Christ. But it is not easy to help people realize how great Christ is in a practical way. "Brother," she said, "I know that the Lord is so great; I know it quite well." So I said, "Sister, I am quite familiar with your problem, and I thank the Lord for what you have always experienced. Tell me, how have you been sustained, how have you been able to stand through all these years?" "Oh," she replied, "it is the Lord! Without the Lord I could never have made it." Then I said, "Sister, do you think the Lord is so limited? If the Lord could help you get through in the past years with one husband and five children, can He not help you make it with one or two children more? Is the Lord so small, so restricted?" Then she understood. "Brother, of course, the Lord is unlimited, the Lord is unlimited!" she exclaimed. I said, "Sister, good! As long as you know the Lord is unlimited, that is sufficient. Be at peace and cast all your burden upon Him. Take the Lord as your unlimited help."

Another time a brother came to me and said, "Brother, my wife is such and such a person. I fear that matters will get worse and worse. I have been able to bear it until now, but if something else happens, I am afraid it will be too much for me; I will have a nervous breakdown. The very thought is unbearable." Then I answered him in the same way as I did the sister. "Brother, how have you been able to manage during the past years?" "Oh, it was only by Christ!" he exclaimed. Then I said, "Brother, do you think the Lord is limited to this extent? If you would experience Him in a greater way, if you would experience a greater Christ, you must be ready to encounter a worse situation." "Oh!" he cried, "That's just what I am afraid of. It's bad enough now. I would ask the Lord to stop right now!" "Well," I told him, "if this is good enough, you can only know Christ to this extent. If you want to have an increasing experience of Christ, you must be ready to meet a worse situation day by day."

Oh, brothers, *by your experience* you may realize the extent, the expanse, of Christ. By your experience you may realize the spaciousness of Christ. It is unlimited. Christ is good in His unlimitedness.

THE DIFFERENCE BETWEEN OUR GOODNESS AND CHRIST'S

One day a brother came to me, saying, "It is rather difficult for me to understand the difference between our patience, and love and the patience and love of Christ. What is our patience, and what is the patience of Christ? What is our love, and what is the love of Christ?" It was not easy to answer. "Brother," he continued, "how can I know whether I am loving a person with my love or with the love of Christ?" I considered, and then I said to him, "If the love with which you love others is the love of Christ, it is unlimited; it can never be exhausted. If the love with which you love others is your own love, I am sure it will come to an end; there will be a limit to it. Today you will love him, and tomorrow you will love him; in these things you will love him, and in those things you will love him. You will love him one day, the next day, and the third day; you will love him this month, this year, and next year. But I am sure that the time will come when you will love him no longer; your love will be exhausted."

There is a limit to human goodness, but the goodness of Christ is without limit. If your patience has a limit, that patience is not Christ. If you are patient with Christ's patience, the more wrongly you are treated, the more patient you will be. This patience can never be exhausted. Christ is good in His unlimitedness; Christ is good in His spaciousness. With everything of Him, there is no limit and no change.

I think most of us have experienced or seen something of the problems between husband and wife. Sometimes I have seen a husband who appears to love his wife so much. I can always predict that after five years this man will not love his wife; his love will be exhausted. But the love of Christ can never be exhausted. If you love your wife with the love of Christ, it will be unlimited. If you love her with your own love, be assured that the more you love her today, the more you will hate her another day. Praise the Lord, we can love others with the love of Christ. We can say, "Lord, it is not my love, but it is Your love, and Your love is Yourself. I love others with Yourself, I love others in Yourself, and I love others through Yourself. The dimensions of the love with which I love others are the breadth, the length, the height, and the depth of Christ."

That piece of land is good. It is good in its spacious ness. There is no limit to Christ. Oh, brothers, I do not like to speak much about myself, but I can testify that the Christ we experience is an unlimited Christ. During the past thirty years the things which have befallen me have always been increasing. The burden of the Lord's work, the churches, and the co-workers has always been increasing. The problems have never decreased. The burdens, the troubles, the problems, the difficulties have been increasing day by day. But, praise the Lord, by the increase of the burden, I have experienced Christ more and more. I have realized that Christ is without any kind of limitation. There can never be a problem which is bigger than Christ. There can never be a situation which He cannot cover.

I have a handkerchief which is only so big—perhaps twelve inches by twelve inches. It can only cover so much. It can never cover the whole room; it is not big enough. But you must realize that Christ is like a piece of cloth without limit. You cannot tell how broad and how long He is. There is no limit. He can cover anything and every thing. No matter how great a problem may be, Christ can cover it. Christ is good in

His unlimitedness. Christ is good in His breadth and length and height and depth. Christ is such a spacious land for us to experience and enjoy in every situation.

CHAPTER THREE

THE GOODNESS OF THE LAND—
ITS ASCENDANCY

Scripture Reading: Deut. 32:13; Ezek. 20:40-42; 34:13-15; 37:22; Acts 2:32-33; Eph. 2:6; Col. 3:1; Phil. 3:10

We have seen that the land is good in its spaciousness. Because it is spacious, it is good. Now we must see something more about the goodness of the land. In the Scriptures we are told that in this land are the high places of the earth: "He made him ride on the high places of the earth" (Deut. 32:13). So this land is also good for its ascendancy.

THE RESURRECTED AND ASCENDED CHRIST

Most of us are aware that the land of Canaan is a high land. It is at least from 2,000 to 4,000 feet above sea level. It is a land of mountains. The books of Deuteronomy and Ezekiel contain many passages which tell us that the land of Israel is a mountainous and high country.

What does this typify of Christ? In order to answer this question we must look at our map. On one side of the land of Canaan is the Great Sea, or the Mediterranean Sea. On the other side is another sea, the Dead Sea. Thus, on both sides of this land are seas. According to the types of the Scriptures, the seas represent death. This means that surrounding Christ was nothing but death! But out of this death something was raised up. Christ was raised from the dead! So the high land, the land on the mountains, typifies the resurrected Christ, the ascended Christ. Christ was raised up from the dead and exalted to the heavens. He is the One who is resurrected and ascended on high. He is the high mountain. Christ is the high land on the mountains of Israel. Beside Him, outside of Him, there is nothing but death.

When the day of Pentecost came, Peter stood up with the eleven. Let us consider the situation on that day. There was Peter, a fisherman, a little man, a low and apparently worthless man. But on that day when he rose with the eleven to testify and proclaim that Jesus was resurrected and ascended to the heavens, this little man was in a position much higher than the highest rank of this earth. The greatest and most exalted on this earth could not compare with Peter and those standing with him. Why were they so high? How could such as them be so exalted? It was because at the very moment they stood up to speak of the ascended Christ, they were in the ascended Christ. They were not men on this earth; they were men in the heavens. By reading the first few chapters of Acts, you will realize that Peter, John and the others with them were people on the mountain, people in the heavens. They transcended everything on this earth. The high priest, the kings and rulers of the people were all under their feet. They surpassed the highest rank of man because of the ascended Christ and because they were in this ascended Christ. They were walking in Him. They were living on this high mountain, in this high land.

Oh, brothers and sisters, Christ is not only spacious, but He is higher than all; He is transcendent!

THE EXPERIENCE OF THE ASCENDED CHRIST

I believe that most of us have had some experience of Christ in this way. What is this experience? Allow me to share with you a little of mine.

In 1943, because of the work of the Lord, I was imprisoned by the Japanese Military Police. At that time the Japanese Army occupied a large part of the mainland of China, and the city where I was working was under their occupation. During my imprisonment, I was brought up for trial almost every day, both in the morning and in the afternoon. From 9:00 to 12:00 in the morning and from 2:30 to 6:00 in the afternoon I stood before them. You cannot imagine what a dreadful situation it was. I had no help but the Lord, and I had no way to get help but to pray. They put me into solitary confinement, because they feared that some word from me might be sent out. I had nothing to do but pray all the time, but I can testify that the more I prayed, the more I felt that I was in the heavens. I was not in prison; I was in the heavens. When I was brought forth to be put on trial before the officials, I felt much higher than they. I was not under them; I was above them. Why? Because I was in the ascended One. Prison was nothing to me, but Christ was everything to me. Oh, brothers and sisters, in the midst of all their threatening, I was living in the heavens.

After three weeks of this kind of treatment, they could find no fault with me. Their only judgment was that I was a superstitious person. They said, "Mr. Lee, you are possessed with God." One day they called me out of prison to mock me. "Tell us," they demanded, "which is more important, God or the country?" I knew their tactics. If I said that the country was more important, they would no longer judge me a superstitious person, but a patriotic person. They intended to determine whether I was patriotic or not, whether I cared for the country or not. I hesitated. They demanded, "Tell us quickly, quickly!" The more they said "quickly," the more I hesitated. Eventually I told them, "To me, God is first." Then they said, "All right, let God give you your bread today; we won't give you any more food in prison." This was another kind of threat. I just smiled at them and went back to prison.

Soon after, a young Greek was arrested and put into prison, and the military police felt that since this man had no relations in the city and thus would not be liable to communicate anything from me, it would be safe to put us together in the same cell. When dinner time came, the Japanese soldier who distributed the food came to the cell. He could not speak Chinese, so he got my attention and mockingly jabbed his finger upward several times. That meant he would not give me anything and God was supposed to feed me. He passed some bread to that young Greek and left me with nothing. After he went, the young Greek spoke with me and inquired about my situation, so I told him the story. Then he said, "Oh, Mr. Lee, I will not take this food. You take it." "But," I replied, "this is your portion." He said, "You are suffering for Christ. Why should I not share your suffering?" So he compelled me to take the bread and drink the milk.

The next day they brought me out of prison to mock me again. "Did your God supply you with food?" "Yes!" I said. They could do nothing with me. They felt that I was just a superstitious person who cared for nothing but God. Then they said, "All right, we will call in a barber to cut your hair and get some good food from the restaurant for you."

Do you realize what kind of experience this was? This was an experience of the ascended Christ. We are in One who has ascended. When we experience Him, we too are ascended. We are transcendent; everything is under our feet.

Not long after I was released from prison, I became seriously ill with tuberculosis. I was confined to bed for six months of absolute rest, followed by two and a half years of greatly restricted activity for recovery. Outwardly speaking, those days were really dark. But, I tell you, whenever I prayed, I felt that I was not in bed. but in the heavens. Though I was gravely ill, yet when I prayed, I had the sense that I was not in illness but far above it all in the heavens. You do not know what kind of pleasure I had in the Lord in those days. Imprisonment and persecution, then poverty and illness. But, praise the Lord, the ascended Christ was my way! The transcendent Christ was my way to the heavens.

Brothers and sisters, how can we be in the heavens? Just by being in Christ. Christ has ascended. Christ is now the high mountain in this universe. He is the high land. I believe most of you understand now what it means to experience the ascended Christ.

When I was young, I came forth to serve the Lord. I am so grateful to Him that under His sovereign arrangement He put me together with two or three senior co-workers. One of them was Brother Watchman Nee. I received much help from them. One day while I was fellowshipping with one who was a sister, she told me how she had experienced something of the resurrection and ascension of Christ. At that time, about thirty years ago, I was a young man. I did not understand what the resurrection and ascension of Christ had to do with us. Doctrinally speaking, I knew all about the resurrection and ascension, but I did not know the resurrection and ascension in experience. This sister told me how she had many experiences of the

Lord's resurrection and ascension. She said, "Brother Lee, one day I met with trouble. There was no reason why I should have such trouble, but it all came upon me. I went to the Lord," she said, "and prayed, 'Lord, what is the reason for this?' The Lord answered, 'That you might know the power of my resurrection.'" She told me that she did learn something of the power of His resurrection. Under those pressures, those troubles, those hardships, she learned something of the mighty power of Christ's resurrection. Nothing could suppress her or depress her. The more trouble she had, the more she was released. Then she told me that after some time, more serious trouble befell her. She went again to the Lord and said, "Lord, what is this?" Again the Lord gave her the answer, "It is only that you might know the power of my resurrection."

Oh, when I was listening to her testimony, I felt that we were both in the heavens. Not only was she there, but I was there with her. This is the experience of the ascended Christ. Everything is transcended and under our feet. Nothing can depress us.

APPLYING THE ASCENDED CHRIST

Sometimes you say, "Oh, I am quite depressed!" Do you know what that means? It means that you are under the power of death. Whenever you feel depressed in spirit or in heart, it means that you are under the threatening of death, you are under the power of darkness. You must learn how to apply Christ, the ascended Christ, to your situation. You must contact Christ immediately. You must say, "I do not agree to be depressed by any kind of situation. I have the ascended Christ; I am in the ascended Christ." You have to tell the Lord; you have to contact Him. When you contact Him, you will be resurrected, you will be ascended, for the Christ whom you contact is the Christ who has ascended to the heavens. When you contact Him, you will be on the high mountains, not in the valleys. You will be in the high land, far above sea level. The problem is that whenever you feel depressed, you forget Christ; you forget that you have such a Christ who is ascended far above all. You do not apply Him. You do not come to Him. You do not contact Him.

Many times brothers have come to me with their minds filled with trouble. One time a brother in this condition came to me, and after talking with him for a while, I said, "Brother, let us kneel down and pray." He replied, "Brother Lee, I cannot pray; my mind is full of trouble." I am afraid that sometimes you are just like this brother. It was exceedingly difficult to get him to pray. When you are faced with such a brother, you really need strength. Sometimes you will be influenced by him. Since he cannot pray, you will be so depressed by him that you cannot pray either. You will rise up and say, "Brother, what shall we do?" He has come to ask you what he should do, and then you turn to him with the same question. Without Christ, there is no way. I have learned whenever I meet such a situation to exercise my spirit and exercise my faith. I say, "Lord, you are here. I do not agree with this kind of situation. Bind the enemy! Bind the strong man! Release this brother! Release his mind! Make him pray!" We need a fighting prayer. We must fight. Praise the Lord! Whenever you pray such a prayer to contact the ascended Christ, you will release the spirit of others. You will bring them to the heavens. Many people have been released by such prayer. They can pray with tears, "Lord, praise You, praise You! I am released!"

Brothers and sisters, how can you fight the battle within you? I will tell you. The only way is by being in the ascended Christ. In the heavens with this ascended Christ, you can fight against the enemy; the enemy will be under your feet. When you are depressed by Satan, when you have been put under his feet, how can you fight against him? You must realize that you are in the ascended Christ. You are seated in the heavens in Christ.

Listen to what we are told in Ezekiel 34:13-15:

I will bring them out from the peoples and gather them from the countries and bring them into their own land, and I will feed them upon the mountains of Israel by the streams and in all the inhabited places of the land. I will feed them with good pasture, and their dwelling place will be upon the mountains of the heights of Israel; there they will lie down in a good dwelling place, and on rich pasture they will feed upon the mountains of Israel. I Myself will shepherd My flock, and I will cause them to lie down, declares the Lord Jehovah.

In the high land, on the mountains of Israel, the Lord's people enjoyed the streams. The streams represent the streams of the Holy Spirit, the living water of the Holy Spirit. In the ascended Christ, you will sense the streams of living waters flowing within you. Some times you feel dry in your heart and in your spirit. It is simply because you are not applying the ascended Christ. By exercising your faith and your spirit to apply the ascended Christ to your situation, you will immediately sense a living stream within you.

We are also told that upon the mountains the Lord's people have the good pasture, the fat pasture, upon which to feed. What is this? This is the Christ of life. The pasture represents the Christ who is so full of life. You will be satisfied. You will never be hungry. Whenever you feel hungry in spirit, it means that you are not experiencing Christ as the ascended One. If you apply such a Christ to your situation, you will immediately feel satisfied. You will have something to feed upon. You will have the riches of the pasture of Christ as your supply.

Moreover, in this high land you have the place to lie down with the flock. This is rest. Are you restless? Contact the ascended Christ and apply Him. On the mountains of Israel you will find rest.

You will have the living water, you will have the fat pasture, and you will have the good fold in which you may lie. You will have a refreshing drink, you will have rich and sustaining food, and you will have rest. And one thing more, the Lord Himself will be your Shepherd. All this will be experienced in the ascended Christ. If you exercise your faith to apply Christ to all your situations, you will enjoy all these things. You will experience the Lord, not just in knowledge or doctrine but in a very practical way in your daily life.

Furthermore, we are told that on the high land of the mountains of Israel the Lord will accept His people as a sweet savor. They will serve the Lord there, and the Lord will be with them. They will offer their oblations to the Lord, and the Lord will accept them.

> On My holy mountain, on the mountain of the height of Israel, declares the Lord Jehovah, there will the whole house of Israel, all of them, serve Me in the land; there will I accept them and there will I require your contributions and the firstfruits of your offerings with all your holy things. As a sweet savor I will accept you, when I bring you out from the peoples and gather you from the countries among which you have been scattered; and I will be sanctified in you in the sight of the nations. And you will know that I am Jehovah, when I bring you into the land of Israel, into the land concerning which I lifted up My hand to give to your fathers. (Ezek. 20:40-42)

This means that by experiencing Christ as the ascended one, we will be enabled to serve the Lord. Then we will be accepted by the Lord and have excellent fellowship with Him. It all depends upon our experience of the ascended Christ.

SERVING IN THE ASCENDED CHRIST

Many times I have met people who have asked me the same question: "Brother, do you feel that serving the Lord is easy or hard?" I always answer in this way: "It depends upon whether you serve the Lord in yourself or in Christ. If you serve the Lord in yourself, it is very difficult; if you serve the Lord in Christ, it is very easy. In Christ, even the labor of your work is a bed of rest to you. The more you labor in the Lord's work, the more you enjoy the Lord's rest."

I was told by Brother Nee, "Whenever you feel that your work for the Lord is a burden, you must tell the Lord that you will put it down and lie upon it as your bed." Can you follow? To serve the Lord in the ascended Christ is nothing but a kind of rest. The more you labor, the more you rest. The ascended Christ makes all the difference. To serve in Him is to rest indeed.

In 1958 I went to Denmark and met a brother who is a full-time worker. He learned much about serving the Lord.

While I was there I was asked to give a series of messages in his conference. Afterwards he came to me and asked, "Brother Lee, do you worry?" I said, "Brother, why do you ask such a question?" He replied, "I realize that you bear a great burden. You have all the care of the Lord's work in the Far East. You have so many co-workers, and there are so many churches. It is a great work, and there must be many problems associated with it! I would like to know whether you worry about it or not." I said to him, "Brother, look at my face. Does it look like I worry?" He answered, "That's just why I came to you. I thought you must have many burdens, troubles, and problems; you must be one who is worrying all the time. But when I see your face, there is no sign of it. It seems that you don't worry at all." Then I told him, "Brother, praise the Lord, I never worry. It is simply because of Christ. I am in the Christ who has ascended to heaven. I don't know how to worry, but I do know how to praise Him."

Praise the Lord! Praise Christ! I am in Christ! Christ is my high land! I am living in this land! I am walking in this high land! All my troubles, all my problems, all my hardships, and all my burdens are under my feet. They have become my seat. I can rest in all my hardships; I can rest in all my troubles. The more troubles I have, the more I enjoy the ascended Christ. This is the experience of Christ.

You also can have this experience and have it now. Christ is in you, and you are in Christ. But I am sorry to say that many times you forget that you have Christ. You simply forget Him; you do not apply Christ to your situation. Please do not think that I am some kind of special or peculiar person. I am very ordinary. I am as ordinary and as weak as you are. But I have the secret. Whenever I meet with troubles, I say, "Lord, I praise You, here is another opportunity for me to experience You."

Apply Christ to your situation. Then you will experience Christ as the ascended One, and you will know that you have ascended with Him too. In Christ you have ascended to the heavens. Oh, brothers and sisters, what a Savior He is! What a Christ He is to us! What a salvation, what a deliverance! He is the living Christ who has ascended to the heavens!

We must realize Christ to such an extent. We have to praise Him that He is the spacious Christ and He is the ascended Christ.

CHAPTER FOUR

THE GOODNESS OF THE LAND—
ITS UNSEARCHABLE RICHES

(1)

WATER

Scripture Reading: Deut. 8:7; 11:11, 12; Eph. 3:8; John 4:14; 7:37-39; 2 Cor. 6:8-10; Phil. 4:12-13

We will continue to see the goodness of the land. The land is good in many aspects. We have seen that it is good in its spaciousness and its ascendancy. Now we come to the matter which is the greatest—the unsearchable riches of the land. The land is good in its unsearchable riches. It is good in spaciousness, it is good in transcendency, and it is good in unsearchable riches.

First of all, it is rich in water. The land is good in the riches of water. We all realize how important water is to our daily life. I think we can endure several days without eating, but we can hardly pass one day without a drink of water. We need water more than almost anything else. Day by day we need water. If you just give me some water to drink, I can stop eating for three days. But I can hardly stop drinking for even one day.

SPRINGS, FOUNTAINS, AND STREAMS

Deuteronomy says that the land is good in water. Listen to the different terms that are used: "a land of waterbrooks"— that means a land full of streams of waters—and a land "of springs and of fountains" (8:7). Do you understand the difference between fountains and springs? The translation of J. N. Darby says that it is a land "of springs, and of deep waters."

Let me illustrate: Suppose we have a well. With a well, there is always a spring. Underneath, at the bottom of the well, is a spring of water which feeds the well. The water issues from that spring and fills the well, and the well becomes the "fountain" or the "deep waters." Then from this deep water, there flows out a stream. You have the spring, then the deep water which is the fountain, and then the stream.

The spring, the deep waters, and the streams. Brothers and sisters, what is the meaning of these waters? We can immediately turn to the Lord's word for the answer. The Lord said that the water He gives will be in us a well of water, a fountain, springing up unto the life of eternity. These waters are types of the various kinds of supply of Christ's life. The life of Christ as the supply to us is just like the different kinds of waters.

The Lord told us that out of the innermost part of those who believe on Him will flow rivers of living water. What is this? This is the supply of the life of Christ as living water. If you reflect upon your experience and consider it carefully, you will realize that in one aspect Christ is so spacious and exhaustless and in another aspect Christ is transcendent and in the heavens. Then if you view it accurately, you will realize that the supply of the life of Christ is just as living water within you. Many times you are thirsty—not thirsty in your physical body, but thirsty in your spirit. When you come athirst to the Lord and contact Him, you have a certain sense within you. You feel refreshed; you feel watered. When you are thirsty, it means that your spirit, your inner man is dry. But when you contact the Lord Jesus, it is not long before you feel watered and your thirst is quenched. You are refreshed more by this drink than by any physical beverage. Then if you contact the Lord more and more and even moment by moment, you will feel more than watered; there will be a stream flowing forth from within you.

You may ask what I mean when I speak of a stream flowing forth from within you. Do you not have such experiences? When you are dry and thirsty in the inner man, you come to the Lord, you contact Him and you are refreshed. Then the more you contact Him, you are not only watered, but you are

filled, you are full of water. I believe that the moment you
meet a brother, you will say Hallelujah! What is this? It is a
stream flowing forth from within you. Then in the evening
when you come to the meeting, you will come singing; you will
come refreshed. You will immediately offer praise or a prayer,
which will be just like a living stream flowing forth from
within you. All the brothers and sisters will be watered by
your prayer. You can tell them, "Brothers, how good it is! But
this is only a stream. Do you know that there is a spring
within me, and not only a spring, but a fountain of deep
water? I am full of water, so something is flowing forth."

Now you can understand. We have a spring, a fountain,
and a stream. The spring is the source, the fountain is the
storage, and the stream is the flowing forth. We have the
source, the storage, and the flowing forth; the spring, the
fountain, and the stream.

I do believe that you have some experience of this, but I
am sorry that you have little spiritual understanding of these
things. You cannot utter it; you cannot give forth a fitting
praise for this living spring, this deep fountain, and this flowing stream. Oh, if you understood this, I believe your praise to
the Lord in the meeting would be much improved. You would
say, "Lord, how I praise You, there is a spring within me! And
from this spring there is a fountain of deep water! Lord, how I
thank You, I not only have a spring and a fountain, but from
this fountain flows a stream; and not only one stream, but
many streams are flowing forth! Lord, how it waters me! I am
so refreshed! The living streams are always flowing forth
from within me, and I am here to water others."

In this land there is not only one stream, but many streams;
not just one spring and one fountain, but many springs and
many fountains. What does this mean? Sometimes when you
are beset with troubles and trials, you contact the Lord and
receive something from Him. You experience the Lord as a
spring, as a fountain, and as a stream in your trial. What kind
of spring, what kind of fountain, and what kind of stream is
this? Can you give them a name? I believe you can give them
many names. Sometimes you experience Him as a spring of joy,
sometimes as a spring of peace, and sometimes as a spring of

comfort. Sometimes you experience Him as a fountain of love, a fountain of grace, and a fountain of light. At other times Christ is a stream of patience, a stream of humility, and a stream of forbearance to you. You see, there are many springs, many fountains, and many streams. There are many kinds of heavenly supplies.

Since 1950 I have visited Manila almost every year, staying for a few months. The brothers there have always lodged me with a family, all the members of which are older persons; so they feel more free to speak with me, of course, than young people. One day in 1953, after my ministry, we all came home from the meeting hall. One of the older sisters said to me, "Brother, would you please tell me how you could possibly have so much to speak? To tell you the truth, when you first came in 1950, I was amazed by the messages. I thought then that your ministry the next time would be poorer. But I noticed that the second time you came, your ministry was richer; you had even more to give. Then I thought, 'The third time he comes, he will be exhausted; he will have nothing to say.' But, to my surprise, the third time you came, your ministry was even richer than the first two times. Now this is your fourth visit here, and after hearing your message this evening, I cannot say how rich it is. Would you please tell me how you get all these things to speak?"

Do you know what I answered her? I told her, "It is quite simple. There is a stream in me which is connected with the spring in the heavens. You can never exhaust this spring. The more the living water flows out, the more the fresh supply flows in. The more I speak, the more I have to speak. If I stop speaking, it stops coming. This stream is flowing all the time."

Once a brother came to me and asked, "Brother, how can you keep so many things in your mind? I notice that whenever you minister, you don't have any outline before you. How can you remember it all?" I said, "Brother, I don't have a great mentality. I cannot remember so many things. But I tell you, there is a stream within me. When I begin to speak, it flows forth." Then he asked, "How much do you have within you?" "Brother," I replied, "I don't know; I cannot tell. For more than thirty years

I have never been exhausted. It is rather hard for me to repeat a message." There is a stream, a stream of ministry.

This is but one of many streams. There is a stream of wisdom, a stream of understanding, a stream of light, a stream of love, a stream of comfort, a stream of peace, a stream of joy, a stream of prayer, a stream of praise. How many streams are there within you? I do not know how many streams there are within me, and I do not know how much there is in each stream. If we only keep in touch with the living Christ, it is really marvelous. We can love others just as a living stream flowing forth. Our patience is flowing as a stream all the time, and we water others.

What a wonderful Christ we have! What a wonderful source we have! From one aspect you realize that He is spacious. From another aspect you realize that He is transcendent. From this aspect He is rich in water.

THE VALLEYS AND THE MOUNTAINS

Deuteronomy says that these waters are flowing forth from the valleys and the mountains. What is the meaning of this? Obviously, without valleys and mountains no water will be flowing. If all the land is a plain, there will be no flow of water. What are the valleys and the mountains?

In 2 Corinthians 6:8-10 Paul mentions many contrasting things, many mountains and valleys:

Through glory and dishonor, through evil report and good report; as deceivers and yet true; as unknown and yet well known; as dying and yet behold we live; as being disciplined and yet not being put to death; as made sorrowful yet always rejoicing; as poor yet enriching many; as having nothing and yet possessing all things.

"Glory" is a mountain; "dishonor" is a valley. The "evil report" is a valley; the "good report" is a mountain. "As sorrowful"—a valley; "yet always rejoicing"—a mountain. "As poor"—another valley; "yet enriching many"—not only a mountain but a great mountain. Some thought that Paul was a deceiver. But he was as a deceiver and yet true; with the valley there was a mountain. In these verses there are at least nine pairs, nine valleys and nine mountains. These are the places from which the water may flow.

If you are someone without any mountains and valleys, if your life is just a plain, I am sure there will be no water flowing within you. The more you suffer, the more you will have flowing forth. The more you have been abased, the more evil reports are made about you, the more the water will flow.

Many times in the past years evil reports have been issued concerning me. Many times people have come to me and said, "Brother, there is one matter of which I am reluctant to speak." Whenever people speak in this way, it is an evil report. When I hear this, I praise the Lord. I say, "Lord, I praise You, here is another valley; here is a valley for something more to flow forth from within." I have received several good nicknames. Recently I was derisively called "the strongest exponent" of a certain thing. I was given this 'honorable title.' There have been all sorts of evil reports. But, praise the Lord, whenever there is a valley, there must be a mountain. This is certain. I am not afraid of an evil report. I know that after the evil report there will be a good report. The water of life flows forth in valleys and mountains. Oh, the life of Christ is unspeakably wonderful!

Whenever God ordains sorrow for you, be assured that rejoicing will follow. "As made sorrowful yet always rejoicing." "As poor yet enriching many." "As having nothing and yet possessing all things." All these are the valleys and the mountains. "I know also," said the apostle Paul, "how to be abased, and I know how to abound" (Phil. 4:11-12). He learned the secret. He knew how to be filled and how to be hungry. What is the secret? Oh, the secret is that Christ Himself is flowing within! I have learned, I have been instructed, I have been initiated. I know the living Christ that is within me.

All the valleys are the experiences of the cross, the experiences of the death of Christ, and all the mountains are the experiences of the Lord's resurrection. A valley is the cross; a mountain is the resurrection. We must be one who always has some trouble, some valley, but also one who is always on the mountains, always in the experience of resurrection. Whenever there is a valley, there is a mountain. Whenever you experience the death of the cross, you will experience the resurrection. The living waters flow forth from all these experiences.

Let us look more closely at the passage in Deuteronomy 8:7. It says there that the water is "flowing forth in valleys and in mountains." It does not say in the mountains and the valleys, but in the valleys and the mountains. First the valleys, then the mountains. Why? Because the first place you contact the flowing water is in the valleys. Then if you trace that stream up to its origin, you find that it springs from the mountains. The stream is in the valley, but the spring is in the mountains. If you would have something flowing out from within you to water others, you must be in the valleys.

I can never forget a story I heard when I was young. It has helped me greatly. The wife of one of the Lord's servants died when she was very young, leaving eight children behind. He too was quite young, and this ordeal was a fiery trial to him. He suffered and he learned something through it. One day some years later, a brother lost his wife, and there were also some children left behind. This brother could not be comforted by anyone; he was exceedingly depressed by the death of his wife. Then the servant of the Lord came to see him. Immediately upon his arrival, the depressed brother said to him, "Brother, I am comforted, I am refreshed! You lost your wife and there were eight children left. I too lost my wife, but only four children were left. There is something coming out of you which refreshes and comforts me."

If you can experience Christ in times of trouble and trial, how much you will have flowing out to others! How blessedly you will water others! It is not in peaceful times or in happy days that you can do this. It is in the days of sorrow, the days of sickness, the days of trouble. It is by your experience of Christ in these times that you may have the living flow to water others. Each situation of death may bring forth a greater outflow of refreshing water. Not only the mountains but also the valleys; not only the valleys but also the mountains. We need many experiences of the Lord's death and many experiences of the Lord's resurrection; then we will be full of the springs, the fountains, and the streams.

These are indeed sweet verses. It is a good land, a land of waterbrooks, of springs, and of deep waters, flowing forth in the valleys and the mountains. And it is by glory and dishonor, by evil report and good report, as deceivers and yet true, as unknown and yet well known, as dying and yet we live, as sorrowful and yet always rejoicing, as poor and yet making many rich, as having nothing and yet possess ing all things. Try to experience Christ and apply Christ when you are in all kinds of suffering; then you will have something which not only refreshes yourself, but also flows forth to water others. This is but a part of the unsearchable riches of Christ; this is just one item of the riches of the good land. The land is good in the riches of water: in brooks, in springs, and in deep waters, flowing forth in valleys and mountains.

THE EYES OF THE LORD

From where does all this water come? It flows forth in the valleys and the mountains. But from where do the valleys and mountains get the water? Deuteronomy 11:11-12 says of this land that "by virtue of heaven's rain, it drinks in water." The mountains and the valleys are not the source. Heaven is the source! All the living waters, all the streams, come from heaven. The source is in heaven. Why does it come from heaven? We are told in this same passage that this land is a land after which the Lord is seeking: "A land which Jehovah your God cares for [Heb.—seeks after]." God is seeking after this piece of good land. "The eyes of Jehovah your God are upon it, from the beginning of the year even to the end of the year." Oh, you can realize, when you are contacting Christ, when you are enjoying and experiencing Christ so that His life is flowing forth from within you, what a deep sense of the presence of God you will have! The presence of God will be so real to you. You will realize that you are one after whom God is seeking and one for whom God is caring. You will experience His eyes upon you from the beginning of the year to the end of the year simply because you are in Christ, you are enjoying Christ, and you are experiencing Christ. Because you are practically joined with Christ, you will not only experience Christ as the living water, but you will enjoy the presence of God. The eyes of God will be upon you all the time. What God is seeking after is this piece of good land. You have to live within this good land and enjoy its riches; then you will obtain the presence of God with the eyes of God.

When you are not happy with me, you turn your eyes away from me. God does the same. But when you are enjoying Christ as such a land, the eyes of God will be upon you from the beginning to the end; you will enjoy God's presence continually. The presence of God will be with you because you experience Christ as your living water, because you are in the good land.

The land is rich in waters. It is a land of water brooks, springs, and deep waters, flowing forth in the valleys and the mountains.

CHAPTER FIVE

THE GOODNESS OF THE LAND—
ITS UNSEARCHABLE RICHES

(2)

FOOD (1)

Scripture Reading: Deut. 8:8-10; 32:13, 14; Num. 13:23, 27;
14:7, 8; Judg. 9:9, 11, 13; Zech. 4:11, 14; Hosea 14:6, 7; John
12:24; 6:9, 13; 15:5

We have seen that there are many types of Christ in the
Old Testament, but only one is the all-inclusive type of Christ,
that is, the land of Canaan. This land is frequently referred to
as the good land. The Lord called it "a good land," and once it
was called "an exceeding good land." We have considered how
good it is in many aspects, such as its spaciousness, its transcendency, and its unsearchable riches. We have seen how
rich it is in water, and now we will see its riches in various
kinds of food.

The Lord in the Gospel of John said that He would give us
the living water, and in the same Gospel He told us that He is
the bread of life from heaven. He not only gives us the living
water, but He is also the bread of life. Something to drink
always accompanies food. If I invite you to a meal, I will give
you something to drink, and I will also give you something to
eat. Food and drink always go together.

Now you can understand why Deuteronomy 8 has such an
order. It speaks first of water, several kinds of waters—
springs, fountains, and streams. The waters are different not
only in their stages, that is, the stage of the spring, the stage
of the fountain, and the stage of the stream, but also different
in various kinds of springs, fountains, and streams. We have

already considered these. Then immediately after speaking about the waters of the land, it speaks about the food.

SEVEN KINDS OF FOOD

The matter of the food has much more detail. Let us look at verse 8:

A land of wheat and barley and vines and fig trees and pomegranates; a land of olive trees with oil and of honey.

There are six items, all of which belong to the vegetable kingdom, and a seventh which is quite peculiar—honey. It seems that honey belongs partly to the animal kingdom and partly to the vegetable kingdom, for it is produced by bees; there is a mingling together of the two kingdoms. Let us name the various items: wheat, barley, vines, fig trees, pomegranates, olive trees, and honey. There are two kinds of grain, four kinds of trees, and honey. The first tree, the vine, produces wine, and the last tree, the olive, produces oil; so we have wine and oil. The second tree produces figs; figs were taken by the Hebrew people as food. The third tree, the pomegranate, produces a fruit of beauty and of bountiful life. So we have four trees—the vine, the fig, the pomegranate, and the olive—and we have two grains, wheat and barley.

What is the meaning of all these things? It is very easy to find a verse telling us the meaning of wheat. John 12:24 tells us that the Lord Himself is a grain of wheat. So wheat clearly represents the Lord Jesus Himself. What then does barley typify? Barley represents Christ too. I know you are certain what the vine represents. The Lord said that He is the true vine. The Lord Himself is the vine. Then who does the fig tree represent? Without question it is Christ again. And the olive tree also is undoubtedly Christ. All these things—the wheat, the barley, the vine, the fig tree, the pomegranate, and the olive tree—represent Christ. But what aspects of Christ are typified by all these items? We need to spend some time to carefully consider this matter.

WHEAT AND BARLEY

Oh, we must worship the Lord for His Word! He put wheat

first, not the barley or the vine. What aspect of Christ does wheat represent? From John 12:24 we can see that the Lord is a grain of wheat falling into the earth to die and to be buried. The wheat represents Christ incarnated. Christ is God incarnated as man to fall into the earth, to die and to be buried. This is the wheat. It typifies the Christ who was incarnated, the Christ who died, and the Christ who was buried.

Then what does the barley represent? The resurrected Christ! Wheat points to His incarnation, death, and burial, and following this the barley points to His resurrection, the resurrected Christ. How can we prove it? In the land of Canaan, the barley always ripens first; among all the grains, the barley is first. In Leviticus 23:10 the Lord said, "Speak to the children of Israel, and say to them, When you come into the land which I am giving you, and reap its harvest, then you shall bring the sheaf of the firstfruits of your harvest to the priest." When the harvest time came, the firstfruits of the harvest had to be offered to the Lord, and the first fruit was clearly the barley. Now we must read 1 Corinthians 15:20: "But now Christ has been raised from the dead, the firstfruits of those who have fallen asleep." All students of the Scriptures recognize that the first fruits of the harvest typify Christ as the first fruits of resurrection. We can prove by this that barley represents the resurrected Christ.

Wheat represents the incarnated, crucified, and buried Christ. Barley represents the resurrected Christ. These two kinds of grains represent two aspects of Christ, His coming and His going. They represent the Christ coming down to be the wheat and the Christ going up to be the barley. You must pay full attention to these two matters. Have you experienced Christ as wheat? And have you ever experienced Christ as barley? What kind of experience of Christ is wheat? And what kind of experience of Christ is barley?

When Jesus fed the five thousand, he fed them with five loaves made of barley. So many are familiar with the miracle of the five loaves, but very few are aware that those loaves were loaves of barley. This Scripture is really wonderful. If they were loaves of wheat, something would be wrong. But they were not wheat; they were loaves of barley. As barley loaves,

they could feed five thousand people with twelve baskets of
fragments left over. This is resurrection. Christ can only be
rich to us in His resurrection. In His incarnation He is exceedingly limited, but in His resurrection He is so very rich. There
is no limit to Him as the resurrected Christ. As Christ incarnate, He was just one grain, a little Nazarene, a humble
carpenter. But when He came into resurrection, He was unlimited. Time and space and material things could limit Him no
longer. There were five loaves, but in effect there were count-
less loaves. There was enough to feed five thousand, not
counting the women and children, and the remains alone—
twelve baskets full—were more than the original five loaves.
This is barley. This is Christ in His resurrection. Christ in His
resurrection can never be limited.

THE EXPERIENCE OF WHEAT

It is not my object just to give some doctrinal teaching.
My burden is not for that. What I am driving at is the experience of wheat and the experience of barley. Let us consider the
experience of wheat. Brothers and sisters, whenever you are put
into a situation by the Lord's sovereignty in which you are
limited, in which you are pressed, you may experience the
Lord as wheat. When in the midst of that limiting and press-
ing situation you contact the Lord, He is just as a grain of
wheat to you. Immediately upon contacting Him, you can be
completely satisfied with your situation and your limitation.
Oh, that life which is Christ Himself within you is a grain of
wheat. It is the life of the little carpenter, the incarnate One,
the limited One. When in a certain environment in which
you are restricted and suppressed you have a living touch
with Christ, you will say, "O Lord, You are the infinite God,
but You did become a finite man. There is power in You to
suffer any kind of limitation." You will experience Christ as
the wheat.

One day a very good and spiritual sister came to see me.
She had come from a rich family and had married a brother
who had to take care of his mother. The mother was amiable
to the son, but to the daughter-in-law it was another story.
This young sister came to me, seeking some fellowship to see

whether her experience was right or not. Then she told me how much she suffered day by day from her mother-in-law. She told me how she went to the Lord and asked the Lord to do something. Of course, she dared not ask the Lord to get rid of her mother-in-law, but she asked the Lord to deliver her from that situation. She said then that when she besought the Lord, the Lord immediately began to show her what kind of person He was on the earth. He showed her how much He was limited as a carpenter in that little family for more than thirty years. When she saw such a vision, she cried with tears, "Lord, I praise You, I praise You! Your life is in me. I am satisfied, Lord, with my present situation. I do not ask You to change anything. I just praise You!" She asked me if her experience was right, and I told her that it was most right. This sister experienced Christ as a grain of wheat. She was really a spiritual sister.

Some time later, this sister came to me again. This time she said, "Oh, brother, praise the Lord, I am not only satisfied with the limitation of my family, but I have seen something more of the Lord Jesus! He was not only limited, but He was also put to death and buried. When the Lord revealed this to me, I told Him that I would not only be content to stay with the situation in my family, but I would even die and be buried in this family for His sake." This was a further experience of Christ as a grain of wheat.

To many of us in many circumstances, the Lord Jesus is just as a grain of wheat. The more we experience Him, the more we realize that He is such a One. He lives in us. He is our life to make us willing to be limited, willing to die, willing to be buried, willing to be nothing. This is the experience of Christ as wheat.

Do you have this experience? What kind of experience do you have? Do you quarrel with your wife or your husband? If so, you are finished with Christ. You must experience Him in such a rich way. You must experience Him both as the living water and as the grain of wheat. If you would look to the Lord when you are so limited and perplexed, I am sure He will show you that He has been limited, put to death, and buried. He will show you that as such a One He lives in you. He will sustain you that you might be limited. He will support you that you might be put to death and buried. He will energize you to such an extent and strengthen you to be such a person. Then you will experience Christ as a grain of wheat.

THE EXPERIENCE OF BARLEY

But is this the end? No! Praise the Lord, following the wheat is the barley. The tomb was not the end of the Lord. He was resurrected! Barley followed the wheat! Wheat is the valley of death, but barley is the mountain of resurrection. Whenever you experience Christ as the wheat, be assured that an experience of Christ as the barley will follow.

Actually, in order to experience Christ as the grain of wheat, the limited Jesus, we must *apply Him* as the barley, as the resurrected Christ. It is the resurrected Christ who is living in us. This resurrected Christ possesses a life which has passed through incarnation, crucifixion, and burial, but He Himself today is the resurrected One. Christ in the flesh is always limited, but Christ in resurrection is unlimited and released. It is this unlimited Christ living in us that causes us to follow the limited Jesus. Today we are following the limited Jesus, but we do it in the power of the unlimited Christ. The unlimited Christ living within us is our enablement.

Let me ask you, when you are in your home or at your job, do you act as the resurrected Christ or as the limited Jesus? If you are a follower of Jesus, you have to be limited. When Jesus was on earth, He was always limited, limited by His flesh, limited by His family, limited by His mother in the flesh and even by His brothers in the flesh. He was always limited. He was limited by space and limited by time; He was limited by everything. If we would live out the life of Jesus, we must also be limited. If we follow His steps, we will have no freedom, no liberty. What a blessing that we can be limited for the sake of Jesus!

But what is the energy for us to be limited? The strength enabling us to be limited must indeed be great. It is easy to be angry, but patience requires strength. It is easy to lose our temper, but longsuffering demands the energy of heaven. The power which enables us to be limited is the power of His resurrection. I need the resurrected Christ living in me in order to be strengthened for just a little patience. To apply the resurrected Christ as my patience is to experience Christ as the barley.

Perhaps you will say to me, "Brother, I know I have to be limited all the time. I must be limited by my wife, by my children, by my boss, by the brothers, and especially by a certain brother. I am limited by this, and I am limited by that; all day I am limited. And I expect tomorrow and the next day to be worse. How can I meet the situation? I realize that the resurrected Christ is living in me, but I have so little of Him. I don't even have five loaves; I just have one loaf." Yes, you may only have one loaf, but remember, it is a barley loaf, it is a loaf of the resurrected Christ who can never be limited. It seems that you just have a little, but it does not matter, because He has no limitation. A little is more than adequate to meet the situation. You say you cannot meet the situation. Right! *You* surely cannot. But there is One who can—the One who is the barley. A barley loaf is within you; a little bit of the resurrected Christ is in you—that is good enough. The resurrected Christ is unlimited. Apply *Him* to the situation. He can never be exhausted. By the power of the resurrected Christ you can follow the steps of the incarnated Jesus. With the life of the resurrected Christ, you can live out the life of the limited Jesus.

Sometimes a brother says, "Oh, I feel burdened to give a testimony, but I am so weak!" It seems that the need is for five thousand people to be fed, but the supply is only five loaves of barley. Nevertheless, you have to go ahead by faith. Though your portion is seemingly so small and the demand is so great, you must realize that what you have is nothing less than *the resurrected Christ*. You can do all things by Him who strengthens you, because He is resurrected and knows no limit. Apply Him!

When a brother comes to see you, remember that Christ is within you as the barley. You have to apply Him in your fellowship with this brother. Sometimes you just forget this. When you meet the brother, you talk about Vietnam, about the world situation, or about the weather. You remember the weather, but you forget Christ. You fail to apply Christ in your fellowship with the brother. When he leaves, you feel hungry, and not only hungry, but sick—sick from not applying Christ. You have to grasp every situation as an opportunity to apply Christ. Apply Him and apply Him and apply Him. Then when you come to the meeting, it will be very easy for you to give praise or a testimony; you will have many loaves of barley to offer to the Lord.

Brother Watchman Nee once told us that when some young co-workers come to a meeting, they look around to see if any senior brothers are there. If not, if all the attendants are new believers, they have the boldness to pray and exhibit what they have. But if they see some senior brothers there, they shrink back with fear. This is not something of the resurrected Christ. If you have the resurrected Christ, even if the apostle Paul were there, you will say, "Praise the Lord, my brother has the resurrected Christ, and I have Him too. He may have five hundred loaves, but I have at least one loaf. Hallelujah!" As long as you have a little bit of the resurrected Christ, you have more than enough to meet every situation. He is the loaf of barley; He is the resurrected One. Nothing can hinder Him; nothing can limit Him.

When you come to the meeting with the brothers and sisters, you must realize your responsibility. You must share in the meeting with others. You must give some thanks and praise; you must offer some prayer. This is your responsibility. You say, "Oh, I am too weak!" In yourself you are weak, but in Christ you are not weak. You say, "I have nothing." Yes, you have nothing, but in Christ you have everything. You say, "Oh, I am too poor!" Yes, you are poor in yourself, but you are not poor in the resurrected Christ. Remember that Christ is the barley in you. When you come to the meeting, apply Him as the one loaf of barley to feed all the others by your prayer or by your testimony. Try it! Practice it! You will see how enriched you will be. Originally you had only one loaf, but eventually you may well have one hundred loaves. You will be enriched by practice. Never say that the meetings are not your business. If so, the meetings are finished. You must learn to apply Christ; you must make use of the Christ you have.

Jesus said to His disciples, "You give them something to eat." The disciples said, "There is a little boy here who has five barley loaves and two fish; but what are these for so many?" The Lord replied, "Bring them here to Me" (Matt. 14:16, 18; John 6:9). As long as they are barley loaves, as long as they are something of the resurrected Christ, that is good enough; that will meet the situation and there will be a surplus.

Brothers and sisters, if you will take my word, believe in the resurrected Christ, and apply Him, you will find that the remainder abiding in you is more than that with which you started. This is the barley. This is not just a teaching, but something for us to experience and apply every day in every situation. Apply the resurrected Christ, the unlimited, inexhaustible One. Tell Him, "Lord, I cannot meet the need, I cannot face the situation, but how I praise You, *You* can. I go ahead trusting wholly in You, counting wholly upon You."

After a considerable time, perhaps five or six years, the sister who experienced Christ as a grain of wheat in her family testified of another experience. This time it was Christ as the barley. She testified that her mother-in-law and many of her relatives were brought to the Lord through her. She had become a barley loaf to feed many people. She had experienced Christ in resurrection.

This kind of experience not only causes you to know Christ inwardly as the wheat and as the barley, but by this experience you *become* a grain of wheat, you *become* a loaf of barley. Then you are food for others. You are able to feed others by what you have experienced. So many people were fed by this sister. Whenever she came to the meeting, even without opening her mouth, all the brothers and sisters sensed the ministration of Christ, the ministry of life. When she uttered a prayer, all the spirits and hearts were satisfied. She became a grain of wheat among the Lord's children. And she herself became a loaf of barley to satisfy and feed many people. She experienced Christ as wheat and as barley; so she herself became a grain of wheat and a loaf of barley.

THE VINE

Now let us see something concerning the trees. The first is

a vine tree. What does the vine represent? In Judges 9:13 the vine said, "Shall I leave my new wine, which cheers God and men?" In one sense it depicts the sacrificing Christ, the Christ who has sacrificed everything of Himself. But this is not the main point. The main significance is that out of His sacrifice He produced something to cheer God and man—new wine.

Have you had such an experience of Christ? I believe most of us have had some experience of this kind, but probably we have not paid much attention to it. Sometimes under the Lord's sovereignty we are put into a certain situation in which we must sacrifice ourselves to make others happy and the Lord happy. When in this situation we come to contact the Lord, it is then that we experience Him as the wine-producing vine; we experience Christ as the One who gives cheer to God and cheer to others. Out of this experience we become the vine; we become the producer of something which cheers both man and God. I know you have had this kind of experience. There are different aspects of Christ to meet every need in every situation. Christ is so rich. He is not only the grain of wheat and the loaf of barley, but He is also all the trees, and the first is one which produces happiness for God and happiness for others. If all the brothers and sisters are happy with you, I am sure that to a greater or lesser degree you are experiencing Christ in this aspect; you are experiencing Christ as a wine producer. Christ as the sacrificing lamb lives in you, energizing you to sacrifice yourself for others to bring them cheer.

Several years ago when I was in Taipei, Formosa, a good number of brothers and sisters came and stayed with us to receive some spiritual help. One sister among them was always murmuring, always complaining. When she took a bath, the water was not hot enough; when she ate a meal, the food was too cold. All day long it was "Why this?" and "Why that?" She gave all those who were living with her a headache. No one was happy with her because she simply had not learned to sacrifice herself. She had never learned how to apply the sacrificing Christ to her situation. She herself was not a happy person, and she did not make anyone else happy. She was short of wine. She had no experience of Christ as the wine producer, sacrificing Himself to produce wine for others and for God.

If you experience Christ in this aspect, you yourself will have much wine to drink, and you will be drunken. Then you will be mad with Christ. You should be a person who is drunken and mad with Christ. You should be able to say, "I am so happy, Lord, I am so happy. I don't know what selfishness means; that is a foreign language to me. Day by day I am drinking the wine of Christ."

The most happy person is the most unselfish one. The most selfish people are always the most miserable. They are always crying, "Have pity on me; treat me a little better!" They are just like beggars, begging all the time. The sacrificing one is the happy one. How can we sacrifice? We have no energy to sacrifice, for our life is a natural life, a selfish life. Only the life of Christ is a life of sacrifice. If you contact this Christ and experience His sacrificing life, He will energize you, He will strengthen you to sacrifice for God and for others. Then you will be the most happy person; you will be drunken with happiness. This is the experience of Christ as the vine tree. By this experience you will become a vine to others. All those who contact you will be happy with you, and you will bring cheer to God.

What must be done to the grapes to make them wine? They must be pressed. To make God and others happy, you must be pressed. You rejoice to learn that Christ is the barley, the resurrected Christ within you, and that He is enough to meet every situation. You say Hallelujah! But do not say Hallelujah too easily, for immediately following the barley is the vine. The grapes must be pressed to bring cheer to God and man. You too must be pressed. The more you drink the wine of Christ, the more you will realize that you must be pressed. You must be broken in order to produce something in the house of the Lord to make others happy.

You see the order: first the wheat, then the barley, and then the vine. Our experience proves this. I say again, do not just take these things as a doctrine or teaching. Remember the ways whereby you may realize Christ in different aspects and apply Christ in your daily living.

CHAPTER SIX

THE GOODNESS OF THE LAND—
ITS UNSEARCHABLE RICHES

(3)

FOOD (2)

Scripture Reading: Deut. 8:7, 8; 7:13; 32:13, 14; Judg. 9:9, 11, 13; Ezek. 34:29; Num. 13:23, 27; Zech. 4:12-14

We have seen three items of the foods in the good land of Canaan: the wheat, the barley, and the vine. Let us notice again the order: first the wheat, then the barley, then the vine. The incarnated, limited, crucified, and buried Jesus comes into our experience first; then we touch the resurrected Christ. By the power of His resurrection we can live the life He lived on this earth. By the resurrected Christ, we can live the life of the incarnated and limited Jesus. Then we learn that the more we enjoy Christ, the more we must suffer. The more we experience Christ, the more we will be put into the wine-press. We will be pressed that something may be produced to please God and others. Our experience testifies to all these things.

THE FIG TREES

We now come to the fourth item—the fig trees. Judges 9:11 tells us that the fig tree represents sweetness and good fruit. It speaks of the sweetness and satisfaction of Christ as our supply. In the first item, the wheat, we could not see the sweetness and the satisfaction; neither could we in the barley. Even in the vine, the emphasis is not on the sweetness and satisfaction of Christ as our supply. We must come for this to the fourth item, the fig tree.

From our experience we realize that the more we enjoy Christ as the wheat, as the barley, and as the vine, the more we experience the sweetness and the satisfaction of Christ. The more we enjoy Christ as the resurrected One, the more we will be pressed, the more we will enjoy Him as the vine. But, praise the Lord, at that very moment we realize the sweetness and the satisfaction of Christ as our supply.

About thirty years ago in China, a young girl who lived in the northern province of Kiang-Su was sick. It was a time of famine, and she was in terrible poverty. In her sickness she was brought to the Lord, and in the face of strong opposition from her entire family she made swift progress in her spiritual growth. Just at that time her husband died, and pressure upon pressure came upon her. She was put into one winepress after the other. Concerning doctrine she knew very little, but she really experienced something in the spirit. She experienced Christ. Day by day she enjoyed Christ and testified that Christ was her very life. Her family was severely antagonistic. The more she attended the meetings, the more her mother-in-law beat her and persecuted her. She sang hymns of praise to the Lord, but the more she rejoiced, the more the wrath of her mother-in-law was stirred, and she was smitten all the more. The sister, however, was undaunted. Her mother-in-law's beatings only caused her to praise her Lord more than ever. One day when she returned singing from the meeting, her mother-in-law was deeply irritated. "Whatever are you doing!" she exclaimed. "We are so poor, and yet you have the heart to sing something!" And upon that, she gave her a good beating. Going to her room and shutting the door, the young sister sang praises to the Lord and prayed with a loud voice. The mother-in-law could not help but hear her and came to the door to listen. "What in the world is the matter with her," the mother thought. "Perhaps she is mad." She listened carefully. Do you know what that young sister was praying? "O Lord, praise You, praise You, I am so happy! Forgive my mother-in-law! Save her, Lord, save her! Give her the light and give her the happiness I have! Bless her, Lord!" All these simple words of prayer greatly surprised the mother-in-law. She thought the young girl was probably cursing her, but instead of cursing, she was praying for her. The mother-in-law knocked on the door. Trembling with fear, the young sister thought that her mother-in-law was coming to beat her again. But instead the mother-in-law asked, "Daughter, how are you, how are you? I beat you! Why do you pray for me, asking your God to bless me and give me joy? What is the matter with you?" "O Mother," the young sister replied, "Christ satisfies me! I am so satisfied. I am full of sweetness. You know, mother, the more you beat me, the more sweetness and satisfaction I have." Immediately the mother-in-law came in and took her hand, saying, "Daughter, let us kneel down. Teach me how to pray. I want to take your Jesus as mine."

Oh, the sweetness and satisfaction of the Lord as our supply! The more we are pressed, we may be sure, the more we will be satisfied. The pressure only causes us to realize His sweetness and His satisfaction. This is Christ as the fig tree.

THE POMEGRANATES

We come now to the fifth item, the pomegranates. What do they represent? Have you ever seen one? When you see a ripe pomegranate, you immediately realize the abundance and the beauty of life.

Consider the young sister we have mentioned. What beauty there was in her life! Her life was the transfiguration of the life of Christ. And what abundance of life there was! One of our co-workers went to that place and became acquainted with her situation. He brought us word that all the churches in that area were nourished by her experience. Praise the Lord for such abundance of life!

When you enjoy and experience Christ as the wheat, as the barley, as the vine, and as the fig tree, the beauty of Christ is about you, the abundance of the life of Christ is with you. This is the experience of Christ as the pomegranate. If you enjoy Christ as the resurrected One and by the power of His resurrection you live the life of Jesus on this earth to suffer all kinds of pressure, persecutions, troubles, and conflicts, you will realize the sweetness and satisfaction of Christ within you, and you will manifest the beauty and the abundance of life to others. When others touch you, they will sense the loveliness and attractiveness of Christ, and an abundance of life will be imparted to them.

THE OLIVE TREE

The sixth item is the olive tree. The olive tree, we know, is the tree which produces olive oil. This is the last item of the foods which we may classify as vegetables. Why has the Spirit put this one last? We have read Zechariah 4:12-14. In that passage there are two olive trees before the Lord, which, the Lord explains, are the two sons of oil. We must realize that Christ is the Son of oil; Christ is the man anointed with the Holy Spirit of God. God poured upon Him the oil of gladness. He is a man who is full of the Holy Spirit; He is the olive tree, the Son of oil. Oh, if we enjoy Him as the wheat, as the barley, as the vine, as the fig tree, and as the pomegranate, we will certainly enjoy Him as the olive tree, which means that we will be filled with the Spirit. We will be full of oil, and we will become an olive tree.

For what purpose is the oil of the olive tree used? We are told in Judges 9:9 that it is used to honor God and honor man. If we would honor God or man, we must do it by the olive oil. This simply means that if we would serve the Lord, if we would help others, we must do it by the Holy Spirit. We must be a man filled with the Spirit, an olive tree, a son of oil. We can never serve the Lord or help others without the Holy Spirit. But praise Him, if we enjoy Him as the wheat, the barley, the vine, the fig tree, and the pomegranate, we will surely have the oil. We will be filled with the Holy Spirit. We will be truly able to honor God and others.

I like the word *honor*. We must not only honor God, but also honor others. Do not think it is a light or superficial matter. Do you realize that whenever you go to contact a brother or a sister, you are going to honor him? By what will you honor him? By yourself? By your natural life? By your old man? By your worldly knowledge? You can only honor him by the Holy Spirit. But you have to be filled with the Holy Spirit. You have to be a son of oil. You have to experience Christ as the olive tree.

Now you can realize why the Holy Spirit has made the

olive tree the last item. When you have experienced Christ as all the other items and have reached this point, then you are full of the Holy Spirit. Then you can honor God and you can honor others.

One day a brother came to visit me, but he did not come to honor me. Do you know what he said? He said, "Brother, today I went to see a movie; it was the best movie I have ever seen! I was so happy that I came to see you." I simply felt that he dishonored me. He put me to shame. He came to dishonor me by a movie instead of honoring me with the Holy Spirit.

Brothers and sisters, if anyone comes to fellowship with you in the Holy Spirit, you are truly honored by that one. That person through the Holy Spirit bestows true honor upon you. Only when we are filled with the Holy Spirit can we honor others. Otherwise, whatever we say, whatever we do, will simply dishonor them. If we can only talk with them about the world situation and about this and that, we are heaping dishonor upon them. In all your contacts with others, can you say that by the Lord's mercy and grace and by the Holy Spirit you honor them? Or do you dishonor them with so many things? To honor others, we must be filled with the Holy Spirit.

Whether or not we are filled with the Spirit to honor God and others depends very much upon how we enjoy and experience Christ day by day as the wheat, the barley, the vine, the fig tree, the pomegranate, and then the olive tree. If we pass the first five items, we will surely come to the sixth, the olive tree. We will be a son of oil, a saint full of the Holy Spirit.

THE ANIMAL LIFE

Now let us go on to see something concerning the animal life. Oh, the aspects of Christ in the land are so many and rich! We not only have the vegetable life, the plant life, but also the animal life. There are two kinds of life. With the Lord Jesus Christ, there is the aspect of the vegetable life and the aspect of the animal life.

The vegetable life is the life that generates, that multiplies. It is the life that is always generating and multiplying. A grain of wheat falls into the ground; it dies and is buried. What happens? Thirty, sixty, or one hundredfold of fruit will be produced. This is generation; this is multiplication. Therefore, the aspect of the Lord Jesus Christ which is represented by the vegetable life is that of generating and multiplying. This is one aspect.

But there is another aspect. We must remember that before the fall, before man had sinned, the food which God ordained for man was of the vegetable kingdom, not the animal. It was after the fall, after man had sinned, that for his diet the blood must be shed. Animals were not required for human consumption before the fall, but when sin entered, man must include them in his food. Without sin, there was no need of redemption through the blood, but after the fall, because of sin, the blood was required. If we are going to live before God, we must partake of redemption through the blood. What then does the animal life signify? It signifies the redeeming life, the sacrificing life. After man fell and sinned, such a life was required that he might live before God.

These are the two aspects of the Lord's life. On one hand, His life is a generating life, and on the other hand, His life is a redeeming life. The Lord said in John 6, "My flesh is true food, and My blood is true drink," and "he who eats My flesh and drinks My blood has eternal life" (vv. 55, 54). We have to enjoy Christ as the redeeming One.

Perhaps by now you feel that you have learned something. You have learned how to apply Christ as the wheat, as the barley, and as so many kinds of trees. You rejoice. But you must realize that you can never simply apply Christ as the barley, because you are a sinner, you have sinned. To this very day, you and I are sinners. Whenever we would apply Christ as the wheat, as the barley, as the vine, as the fig tree, as the pomegranate, and as the olive tree, at the same time we must apply Him as the lamb, as the One who died on the cross, shedding His blood to redeem us from our sins. With all the offerings in the Old Testament, there was always the offering of an animal with the offering of the vegetable. You know what Cain did. He offered vegetables without something of an animal, and he was rejected by God. Whenever you would enjoy Christ, you must realize that you are sinful. You must ask the Lord to cover you with His precious blood and cleanse you once more. You cannot simply enjoy Christ as the plant, as the wheat or as the barley. You have to enjoy Him as the plant *with* the animal. You must enjoy Him as the generating life and at the same time as the redeeming life.

One day a couple, a brother and a sister, came to see me. They said. "Brother, we know your stomach is not so strong, so we have prepared some food for you. We would like to invite you to come to our home for dinner." I replied that I was so willing to do so. When I went there, they had indeed prepared some good food, and they had prepared it very nicely. When they spread the table, it was quite colorful. There was the green, the red, the white, and the yellow—it looked most pleasing. But I shook my head. My wife noticed and asked, "What is the matter? Why are you shaking your head? Don't you like this food?" "I like it," I said, "but it is not scriptural; there is nothing of the animal." All that was prepared was of the plant life. There were vegetables, vegetables, and more vegetables, and some fruit, but there was no meat. There was nothing of the animal. "Do you think that I am not a sinner?" I asked the sister. "Do you think that I do not need to take the Lord as the slain One, that I do not need His blood at this very moment?"

Now you understand. You cannot simply experience Christ as the plant life, as the vegetable life. You are sinful. Whenever you offer the meal offering, you must also offer something of the animal. Whenever you take Christ as your life, as the wheat, as the barley, as the fig, or as the pomegranate, you must at the same time take Him as the bullock or as the lamb. He is the One who was slain on the cross, shedding His blood to redeem us from our sins.

One day a brother came to me, saying, "Brother, whenever I hear you pray, you always say, 'Lord, cleanse us with Your precious blood that we may enjoy You more and more.' Why do you always ask the Lord to cleanse you with His blood?" "Brother," I answered, "don't you realize that you still have a sinful nature? Don't you realize that you are still living in this corrupt and defiling world? Are you not defiled from morning to evening by many things?" Whenever we come to experience Christ and apply Him as our life, we must realize that He is not only the plant life, but also the animal life. We must always apply Him as the redeeming One, as the Lamb who has been slain, that we may enjoy all the riches of His generating life.

MILK AND HONEY

Now we come to two more items—milk and honey. The good land is a land flowing with milk and honey. Can you tell to which life the milk and the honey belong? Do they belong to the animal life or to the vegetable life? Notice how the Holy Spirit arranges them in the Word. In Deuteronomy 8:8 the honey is put with the plants: the wheat, the barley, the vine, the fig tree, the pomegranates, the olive tree, and then the honey. And in Deuteronomy 32:14, the milk is put with the animals: the cattle, the flock, the milk, and the butter. The Holy Spirit is very fair. He put the honey with the plants, and He put the milk with the butter and the animals. Why? Because the Holy Spirit is well aware that for the most part, honey has to do with the plant life. It is derived mostly from the flowers and the trees. Of course, a part of the animal life is involved—that little animal, the bee. Without the flowers we cannot have honey, and without the bees we cannot have honey either. We must have flowers and we must have bees. These two cooperate; these two lives are mingled together, and honey is produced. But honey, for the most part, belongs to the vegetable life.

What about the milk? We can say that the greater part of milk belongs to the animal life. But indeed it is the product of both the animal life and the vegetable life. If we do not have the pasture, if we do not have the grass, even though we have the cattle and the flock, we cannot have milk and butter. Which is the better food: the milk, or all the fruit of the trees—the vine, the fig, the pomegranate, and the olive? Yes, they are all good, but which is better? I believe we all realize that milk is better than all the fruit of the vegetable life. Why? Because with both milk and honey, we enjoy the mingling of two kinds of life. You see then that both these items are of the vegetable and of the animal lives.

What is the meaning of this? What aspects of the life of Christ do the milk and the honey portray? When you enjoy

Christ as the wheat, the barley, the vine, etc., and at the same time you enjoy Him as the bullock and as the lamb, you will realize that the Lord is so good, that the Lord is so sweet and so rich to you, just as milk and honey. Especially when you are weak in spirit and you come to the Lord to experience and apply Him, you sense that He is the milk and the honey. You sense the riches and the sweetness of the life of Christ. Oh, the goodness of milk and the sweetness of honey! Christ is so good! Christ is so sweet! He is a land flowing with milk and honey. This experience is produced from the two aspects of the life of Christ, the generating and the redeeming life. The more you realize Him as the wheat and the barley and so forth, and at the same time as the cattle and the flock, the more you will enjoy Christ as milk and honey.

We have seen three kinds of waters and at least eight kinds of food. Oh, how rich Christ is to us! We must have such an adequate and full experience of Him, not just as the living water, but as so many kinds of food. We must enjoy Christ to such an extent that the life within us may be matured. Then there will be a building for the Lord and the warfare with the enemy. We will consider this in the next chapter.

CHAPTER SEVEN

THE GOODNESS OF THE LAND—
ITS UNSEARCHABLE RICHES

(4)

MINERALS (1)

The land is not only rich in water and food but also rich in minerals. Let us read:

Deuteronomy 8:9: A land whose stones are iron, and from whose mountains you can mine copper.

Please notice here that the iron is put together with the stones, and the copper, with the hills. This means that the iron has something to do with the stones, and the copper has something to do with the hills or the mountains.

Genesis 4:22: The forger of every cutting instrument of bronze and iron.

Bronze and *copper* are words used interchangeably for the same material in the Old Testament. Here the bronze and the iron are related to cutting instruments.

Deuteronomy 33:25: Your doorbolts shall be iron and copper; / And as your days are, so shall your strength be.

Here the bronze and the iron are related to the doorbolts of the gates and also to strength. The footnote in the American Standard Version gives "rest" or "security" for the word *strength* in this verse. Really the word *security* is better. As your days are, so shall your security be. Iron and bronze, therefore, are here related to our security. If you have strength, you have security, and if you have security, you have rest.

Jeremiah 15:12: Can one break iron, / Iron from the north, or bronze?

This verse shows the strength of iron and bronze. It means that no one can break iron and bronze.

> 1 Samuel 17:5-7: There was a bronze helmet upon his head; and he was clothed with scaled armor, and the weight of the armor was five thousand bronze shekels. And he had bronze greaves upon his legs and a bronze javelin slung between his shoulders. And the shaft of his spear was like a weaver's beam, and the head of his spear weighed six hundred iron shekels.

This giant warrior was covered from head to feet with bronze, and his weapon was made of iron. He himself was covered with bronze, and the weapon with which he fought the battle was of iron.

> Revelation 1:15: His feet were like shining bronze, as having been fired in a furnace.

> Psalm 2:9: You will break them with an iron rod; / You will shatter them like a potter's vessel.

In Revelation 1 the bronze is related to the feet of the overcoming and judging Christ: His feet were like burnished bronze. And in the second Psalm the iron is related to the rod with which the Lord will rule the nations.

> Matthew 5:14: You are the light of the world. It is impossible for a city situated upon a mountain to be hidden.

> Psalm 2:6: I have installed My King / Upon Zion, My holy mountain.

In Matthew 5 the city is related to the hill, and in the second Psalm the hill of Zion is related to the anointed One.

> 1 Peter 2:4-5: Coming to Him, a living stone, rejected by men but with God chosen and precious, you yourselves also, as living stones, are being built up as a spiritual house into a holy priesthood to offer up spiritual sacrifices acceptable to God through Jesus Christ.

Here we are told that the Lord is a living stone and that we too are living stones. All these living stones are for the building of a spiritual house for God.

> Ezekiel 37:22: I will make them one nation in the

land upon the mountains of Israel, and one king
will be king to all of them.

In this verse we see that the nation and the king are related
to the mountain. The Lord said that He would make them a
nation not only in the land but also on the mountains of
Israel, the mountains of the land.

Psalm 87:1: His foundation is in the holy mountains.

Here the foundation of the building is related to the mountains.

Psalm 48:1-2: Great is Jehovah, / And much to be
praised / In the city of our God, / In His holy mountain. / Beautiful in elevation, / The joy of the whole
earth, / Is Mount Zion, the sides of the north, / The
city of the great King.

We must notice here that the city of God is related to the holy
mountain, and the city of the great King is related to Mount
Zion.

There is much spiritual significance in all these rela-
tionships. There are four items altogether: stones, hills or
mountains, iron, and copper. The stones are for the building,
and the hills or the mountains are for the city which is the
center of the nation, the center of the kingdom. The iron and
copper are the materials for the weapons.

FOUR CATEGORIES OF RICHES

We have seen that the land is rich first in waters, second
in vegetables and plants, third in animals, and last in mines
or minerals. There are four categories. Let us consider their
order—it is very meaningful and very spiritual.

We must have water first; otherwise, the plants cannot grow.
Without water, plants and vegetables can never exist and
never grow. So water brings in the vegetables and the plants.

In 1958 we went to the physical land of which we are
speaking, the land of Palestine. After staying in Jerusalem for
a few days, we went to see Jericho, that cursed city. Jerusalem
is built on a mountain, from three to four thousand feet above
sea level, and the valley of Jericho, where the Dead Sea is
located, is six to seven hundred feet below sea level. So from

Jerusalem to Jericho's "Death Valley," we went down, down, down—a drive of about three hours. When we arrived at the bottom of that valley, it was like a furnace. Oh, the heat! And there was no breeze! It was a burning, barren wilderness— just heat and dust. We went immediately to see the remains of the ancient city of Jericho in the midst of that bleak and arid scene, and just outside the city, to our delight, was water, a spring of water. It was the very water that was healed by the prophet Elisha, and because of this we were very interested in seeing it. There it was—a spring, a fountain bubbling up, and a stream flowing forth. Following the water with our eyes, we could see at a distance, in the midst of that wild valley, a place of green grass, palm trees, and many other kinds of trees. It was beautiful. You see, there were the spring, the fountain, the stream flowing forth, and then a land full of green.

The Holy Spirit put the water first. The spring, the fountain, and the stream bring in all kinds of plant and vegetable life.

Then what do the cattle feed upon? They feed upon the vegetables, upon the plant life. So you see the order: first the waters, then the vegetables, then the animals. After these three, the Spirit turns to something else—to the stones and to the mountains, out of which the iron and the copper come.

Brothers and sisters, we must be deeply impressed with this order. It corresponds one hundred per cent with the stages of the spiritual life.

THE STAGES OF THE SPIRITUAL LIFE

In the first stage of the spiritual life, we experience Christ as the living water. Jesus said, "If anyone thirsts, let him come to Me and drink" (John 7:37). This is the gospel for the sinners. Come and drink, and you will be filled; your thirst will be quenched. When we come to the Lord, we experience Him as the living water, as the living stream. By continuing in this experience we are brought further. We are told that from the throne of God and of the lamb, there flows a river of living water, and in this river grows the tree of life. The living water brings us the supply of Christ as food. By experiencing Christ as the living water, you will find growing in this water different kinds of plants; you experience Christ as your food supply. With the flowing of the living water is the bread of life, the food of life. This means that you not only experience the waters but also the supply of Christ as different kinds of food. All these kinds of food will bring you to maturity; they will bring you to the place where you are filled with the Holy Spirit. You will be an olive tree before the Lord, a son of oil.

At this point you are mature. Your experience of Christ is so rich and sweet, just as milk and honey. What is honey? Honey is the cream of all the plant life. And what is milk? Milk is the cream of all the animal life. Milk and honey are the cream of all the food supply. Sometimes when you are weak in spirit and you taste a little of Christ, you sense how rich and sweet He is. You have enjoyed just a little of Christ as milk and honey. But when you are really mature in the life of Christ, Christ will be just as milk and honey to you through the whole day. When you first come to receive Christ, you feel that you are drinking the living water, but when you are matured in Christ, you feel day by day that you are drinking milk and honey. He is so sweet and so rich to you. Of course, the living water is included in the milk and honey, but this drink is exceedingly richer than water.

The first time I came to America, I received a deep impression. I was thirsty and asked the brother with whom I was staying for something to drink. I asked him if he had a teapot, and he replied that he was sorry, but he had no teapot. I exclaimed, "Is America so poor? You don't even have a teapot!" Where I come from, we have all kinds and sizes of teapots. Then I asked him if he had some thermos bottles of water. He replied that he had none of them either. "What is the matter?" I thought. Then to my surprise he gave me a cup of milk, saying, "Brother, here in America we drink milk instead of water. Every day, morning, noon, and evening, we drink milk." I was much impressed. I said, "Oh, you are really rich in this country! You are so rich that instead of water, you drink milk!"

The first experience of Christ is that of living water, but after growing in Him and maturing in life, a certain point is reached where Christ is not only the living water, but the flowing of milk and honey. You must notice the order. The Holy Spirit put honey at the end of the list of the vegetables, and He put the milk and butter after the cattle and the flock, the animals. This means that if you enjoy Christ to a certain extent as the plant life, you will enjoy Him as honey. And if you enjoy Him to a certain extent as the animal life, you will feel that He is just as the milk. He will be so rich and sweet to you. This means that you are somewhat mature.

Now we come to the last stage, the stage of the minerals. We come to the place where we have something to do with the stones, the mountains, the iron, and the copper. What are these for? They are for the building, for the kingdom, for the battle, and for the security. Whenever there is a matured life in Christians, the building of God's house will take place and the battles of the spiritual warfare will be fought. In other words, when there are believers who are matured by experiencing Christ, with them the house of God is built and by them the battle is fought. We must be very clear that whenever we enjoy Christ to a certain extent, there is always an issue— the building and the battle. These two always go together. If you would have the building of God, you must prepare to fight. For the building of God we need the materials, and for the fighting of the battle we need the weapons. All these depend on the stones, the mountains, the iron, and the copper.

We must remember that upon the land, the city and the temple are built, and they are built with these very materials— stones, iron, and copper. These minerals signify that there is something in the life of Christ as materials for the building of God and as weapons for the fighting of the battle. All these things are still something of the riches of the life of Christ.

Whether or not we have arrived at this stage depends upon the measure of our experience of Christ. If we just enjoy Christ as the living water day by day, we can never reach the point where the building of God will be realized among us. We are still very young. We must enjoy Christ as the living water, as the wheat, as the barley, as this and as that. We must enjoy Christ to a certain extent; then there will be a building for the Lord and the battle with the enemy.

Sometimes you meet a brother or a sister, and you feel that he or she is quite good, but there is something short, there is a real lack. It is not that they are sinful; on the contrary, they are upright with the Lord and their attitude is positive. But deep in your spirit you sense a lack. You can hardly explain it; it is difficult to find the right word. Perhaps you could say that they are a little limp, a little soft. I believe you know what I mean. They are just like a piece of bread. The bread is good and wholesome, but how soft and limp it is. Or they could be compared to a cup of milk. The milk is good and rich, but it is only liquid and as weak as liquid. Now take a stone, or a piece of iron or copper—oh, here is something strong! But these people are not like that. It seems that they are not a stone, and no iron or copper is in them. You cannot fight with milk as a weapon. You cannot do battle with a piece of bread or go to war with a fig. How ridiculous! You must have some iron or copper; you must have something of strength. You cannot build a house with milk. You cannot pile up loaves of bread and have a building. You must have stones; you must have building materials. Furthermore, you must have a mountain from which you may quarry the materials and upon which you may build the house.

Sometimes when I meet one of the Lord's servants, I have the feeling that I am meeting a mountain. I cannot tell how rich, how strong, how solid, and how secure he is. He is just like a mountain. When he is sitting there, a mountain is there. You cannot beat him. If you attempt it, you will be beaten by him. This is a mountain, this is a hill. You cannot deal with him; you have to be dealt with by him.

This is the last stage of the spiritual life. It is quite possible for you to come to this point. It is quite possible for you to be a stone among the children of God, a pillar in the church. Can you use bread for pillars? Can you pile up grapes for pillars? No, you cannot do that. You can make a pillar of stone, of iron, or of bronze—that will be quite adequate. The building of God requires the stone, the iron, the copper, and the mountain. All these materials are related to the building of God and, as we will show later, to the kingdom of God.

TRANSFORMED FROM CLAY TO STONE

When we are just babes in Christ, drinking the living water, how is it possible for the building of the Lord to be among us? It is impossible. We must be grown; we must be matured by experiencing Christ. We must be stones. The Lord is the living stone, and we too must be the living stones so that we may be material for His building.

Figuratively speaking, in Adam we are a piece of clay; we are not stone but clay. The Lord's building is built with stones, but we are made of clay. How could we as a piece of clay be material for the Lord's building? It is impossible. We must be transformed from clay to stone. We must be transformed by the Holy Spirit through the practical experience and enjoyment of Christ.

Sometimes a brother comes to me, and I sense that he has been somewhat transformed. But, regrettably, he has only a small amount of stone in him; for the most part he is still clay. You may have met brothers like this. You can recognize a little transformation; they look like a stone, but the greater part of their being is still in the original state. They are still very much in Adam, very much in the clay. They are still too natural.

One day I had fellowship with some brothers. At a certain point in our fellowship, one brother insisted very strongly on a certain matter. I pointed to the brother and said, "Brother, there in your spirit is a little piece of stone, but your head is a piece of clay." The mentality of so many brothers and sisters is still not renewed, not transformed. Their mentality is just that of the natural man, full of natural concepts and natural thoughts. It is a head of clay. By the renewing of the mind we are transformed from a piece of clay to a stone. After becoming a stone, we are burned and pressed that we may be transformed even further—from an ordinary stone to a precious stone. In the New Jerusalem you cannot find one bit of clay. Neither can you find any ordinary stones. Every stone is a precious stone. The New Jerusalem is built with precious stones.

THE MOUNTAINS AND THE HILLS

We know that stones are always related to mountains and

hills. If we want some rocks, we must have some mountains. It is rather difficult to find stones in the plains. Then what is the meaning of the mountains and the hills? The mountains and hills in the Scriptures always represent resurrection and ascension. They are something which is raised above the earth, above the plain. How could you, a piece of clay, be transformed to a stone? Only in the resurrection life! All the spiritual, living stones are in the resurrection life; they are stones joined to the mountain of Christ's resurrection. If we are all living in the Adamic life, in the old life and nature, we are simply in the plain. Since there is no mountain among us, there is no stone among us. But if we are living and walking in the resurrection life, we are enjoying the reality of the hills and mountains, and with these hills and mountains inevitably are the stones.

Let us illustrate. Suppose I meet together with a few brothers and sisters. I as a brother walk according to the natural life, and there is another brother who is always living in the natural life. A dear sister who meets with us is continually walking and living in her emotions: sometimes she is so happy, and sometimes she is exceedingly sorrowful and depressed. In fact, we are all a group of such believers; we are all so natural, continually living and walking in the natural life. Could you sense something in the nature of a hill among us? Certainly not. We are all clay; we are all on the plain. If you looked for a stone, you could find nothing but dust—dust, earth, and clay. Since there is no mountain, there is no stone. If you want stones, you must go to the hill country.

Suppose, then, there is another group of believers. They know something of the cross, they know something regarding the denial of the natural life; therefore, they have realized the resurrection life to a certain extent. They are walking in newness of life and serving in newness of the spirit; they are living in resurrection. When you come to them, you sense there is something raised, something exalted, something which is higher than you. You realize that within them and among them is some spiritual hill, some spiritual mountain. It is not difficult to find many stones, even precious stones. If you look at this one, you see a stone; if you look at that one, praise the Lord, you also see a stone. There are stones because there are mountains and hills.

The mountains and the hills are for the building of the house, the city, and the kingdom of God. So many cities in the Scriptures are built upon hills and mountains. When I was in Palestine and traveled throughout the land, I noticed that nearly all the cities were built in this way. There were very few cities built in a valley or on a plain. A city is the center of a nation, a kingdom. In the Old Testament Scriptures the city was always the symbol of the nation or the kingdom. The thought of the Holy Spirit in such passages, therefore, is that whenever there is some spiritual hill or mountain among the Lord's children, there are automatically some stones, some materials for the building of the house and the city. The authority of God and the kingdom of God are there. When the Lord was raised from the dead, He told us that all authority in heaven and earth was given unto Him. The spiritual authority, the heavenly authority, is always in resurrection. If you and I are living and walking in the resurrection life of Christ, we will have the authority of heaven.

The concept of many people concerning the authority of the church is entirely mistaken. The authority of the church has nothing to do with organization. It is absolutely a matter of resurrection. If two brothers in the local church are so much in the resurrection, to them the divine, the heavenly authority is committed. They are the authority of the church. They are the hill in that local church. With them is the resurrection, so with them is the authority of the kingdom.

If we are just babes in Christ, we have experienced Him as living water and perhaps as our food supply. We are always having good times together and are so happy with each other, but we are very young. Many times we are just naturally happy, and many times we are sorrowful in our natural emotion. There is no hill among us, and there are no stones among us. We are all a lump of clay. Could you realize the authority of the church in such a situation? Never. The authority of the church is where the saints know what it means to be crucified with the Lord Jesus and live in the resurrection. If they laugh, they laugh in resurrection; if they cry, they cry in resurrection. Even when they are angry, they are angry in the life of resurrection. They experience the Lord's resurrection life in their daily walk. It is not a mere teaching to them but a practical daily enjoyment. When you meet them, you feel that they are stones in the mountain. They are the ones to whom the heavenly authority is committed. They are the authority of the church. If the saints are like that here, then the house of God and the kingdom of God are here. Here the house is built up, and the kingdom of God is established.

Please do not think that because you have read this, you have it. What we have been speaking of requires years to obtain. I am only giving you the directions; this is simply the map for you to follow. Take it and humbly practice it. Do not think that tomorrow you will be a mountain. No! Pray about these matters and seek to put them into practice. Then after this, you will be profited.

CHAPTER EIGHT

THE GOODNESS OF THE LAND—
ITS UNSEARCHABLE RICHES

(5)

MINERALS (2)

Scripture Reading: Deut. 8:9; 33:25; Jer. 15:12; Rev. 2:27; 1:15; Matt. 28:18; Luke 10:19; Matt. 16:18, 19; 18:17, 18; Eph. 6:11-17

We have seen clearly that the riches of the land are firstly in waters, secondly in all kinds of vegetables and plants, thirdly in cattle and flocks, and fourthly in mines or minerals. Let us name them in their various categories:

1. Waters: springs, fountains, and streams.
2. Plants and vegetables: wheat, barley, vines, fig trees, pomegranates, olive trees.
3. Animals: cattle, flocks.
   (The mingling together of the above two lives, the plant and the animal, produces the milk and the honey.)
4. Minerals or mines: stones, mountains, iron, copper.

We have seen how all these riches correspond with the various stages of the spiritual life. The living waters belong to the first stage of our spiritual experience. Experiencing Christ in the first stage, we feel He is just as living water to us. Then, in the second stage, we have a further experience of Christ; we enjoy Christ more solidly. Christ is just as the solid food to us; He is something more than water. Water is certainly good and most necessary, but water is not so substantial. I cannot live and grow only with water. If you invite me to dinner, you must give me some solid food, some wheat or some barley, etc. It is indeed wonderful, then, that at the end of the plants and vegetables is the olive tree, representing Christ as the Son of oil, the One who is full of the Holy Spirit. Within and without He was saturated with the Holy Spirit, and we can enjoy Him as such. We can be filled with the Holy Spirit and saturated with the Holy Spirit. When we are so full of the Spirit, we are mature in the life of Christ. Christ is so dear, so sweet, so rich to us, just as milk and honey.

Immediately following such a rich experience of Christ, we come to the mines and the minerals—the stones, the mountains, the iron, and the copper. This is the order of the Holy Spirit. The Holy Spirit put all these items in such an order to correspond with the stages of the spiritual life. When we are mature in the life of Christ, we realize something in our experience of the stone, the mountain, the iron, and the copper.

In the previous chapter we have seen much concerning the stones and the hills. We have seen that the stones represent the saved and transformed saints as the material for God's building. We must not only be saved but also transformed into the living stones for the building of God. Originally we are not stones; we are pieces of clay. But when we accepted Christ, He came into our spirit and has been continually working to transform us. By the renewing of the Holy Spirit, we are transformed from a piece of clay to a stone that we may be material for the building of God.

We have also seen that the hills and the mountains represent resurrection and ascension. With resurrection and ascension is always the authority, the kingdom and the King. Resurrection is something raised up, and ascension is something exalted, and with this exaltation is the divine authority, the divine government, the kingdom of God with the King. This is the meaning of the mountains and the hills. We have seen that the only way for the clay to be transformed to the stone is in resurrection. Only in the resurrection life is Christ able to transform us. In the natural life we are a piece of clay, but in the resurrection life we are a stone. The stones produced for the building of God with the divine authority and government are all the issue of Christ's resurrection. The more we enjoy Christ and experience Christ, the more we will be transformed by the Holy Spirit with the elements of His life. Then the building of God and the kingdom of God will come into view.

IRON AND COPPER

Now we come to the last items, the iron and the copper. I believe you are familiar with the sequence in the Epistle to the Ephesians. The first chapter tells of all the blessings we have received in Christ. Then the second, the third, the fourth, and the fifth chapters are all related to the riches of Christ. This is the only book in which the term *the unsearchable riches of Christ* is mentioned (3:8). After the account of these riches, we come to chapter 6, the end of the book. There we see the battle, the warfare. The last item in the book of Ephesians is the spiritual warfare. By the time you reach chapter 6 of Ephesians in spiritual experience, you have had an abundant enjoyment of the riches of Christ; you have experienced the Christ of chapters 1 through 5. Because you have enjoyed Him to such an extent, and because of the need for the building of God and the divine government, you must fight the spiritual warfare. When you arrive at this point, you will be enabled to fight, you will be qualified to fight, you will be matured in the life of Christ. In the experience of the riches of Christ, you must fight and you can fight.

Immediately upon being brought to the battlefield in this chapter, we read these terms: *helmet, breastplate, shield, sword,* etc. Figuratively speaking, what is the helmet made of? And of what is the breastplate composed? They are certainly not constituted of any soft or fragile material. In the record of 1 Samuel 17 there is a giant warrior covered with bronze. His head, his breast, his knees, and his legs were all sheathed with bronze. And the sword with which he fought was made of iron. The last items of the riches of Christ are iron and copper or bronze, because the last stage of Christian experience is the spiritual warfare. In the battle we need both copper and iron.

What elements of Christ do iron and copper represent? We are told that Christ will rule the nations with a rod of iron. Iron, therefore, stands for the authority of Christ. Christ is the One with full authority over the entire universe. All authority in both heaven and earth has been given to Him. He has been exalted to the heavens, to the right hand of God, and has been made Head over all things. He has the iron. The rod of iron is in His hand. This is quite clear.

Then what aspect of Christ does copper or bronze typify? Bronze stands for the judgment of Christ. But we must realize that all His judging power and judging authority issue from the trials He suffered. When He was here on earth, He passed through all kinds of tests and suffered every kind of trial. His feet are like burnished bronze, refined in the furnace. What do the feet represent? The feet represent the walk, the life on earth. The walk and life of the Lord on earth have been refined, burnished, tested, and tried by God. They have even been tested by the enemy and by humanity. By all these tests, the Lord's life and walk have been proved and come forth perfect, bright, and shining. He has been qualified by this. He has been qualified to judge others, because He has first been tested, judged, and refined. He is equipped not only with bronze but with refined and shining bronze. He has the ground, He has the right, to judge.

APPLYING THE COPPER

How can we apply this? Sometimes when you are following the Lord, while you are serving the Lord, or perhaps while you are coming to a meeting to minister, a thought of how dirty and sinful you are enters your mind. What do you do at such an instant? Yes, you ask the Lord to cover you with His precious blood and cover your mind with Himself. But do you realize what this is? This is the helmet made of bronze. You realize that the Lord is the perfect One, the shining One, the One who has been tested and proved. Then in faith you exercise your spirit and say to the enemy, "Satan, I am dirty, I am sinful; but praise my Lord, He is the perfect One, He is the One who has been tested and proved, and He is my covering, He is the helmet for my head!" You can exercise your spirit by faith to apply this tested, proved, and perfect Christ as the helmet for your head.

Do you have such experiences? I believe you have, but you are not clear regarding them. You must learn how to apply Christ in this way with an enlightened heart.

I know the subtle working of the enemy. More than thirty years ago, when I was a young man, by His grace I loved the Lord greatly. Early every morning I went to a certain mountain to sing hymns, to read the Scriptures, and to pray, many times with tears of love and joy. Oh, the fellowship was so sweet and the presence of the Lord was so full! But when I came down from the mountain, all kinds of thoughts entered my mind. Every morning it was the same. At first I thought something was wrong with me. I confessed to the Lord and asked Him to forgive me. But, praise the Lord, after just a few days, I was clear. I said, "No! This is not something of me. I love the Lord so much, I read His Word and pray, I have had such excellent fellowship with the Lord, how could these things be from me? They must be from the enemy." Do you know what I did? I shook my fist at the enemy. That was my way to fight the battle.

After some time, I learned that there is a helmet for my head, that one of the parts of the armor of God is a helmet. From that time I learned the lesson. Whenever these thoughts came to trouble me, I said, "Lord, cover me with Your helmet. Hallelujah! You are the Victor! Your precious blood is the victorious blood! Cover me, Lord! Praise You, Lord!" I got the victory. Later I understood clearly why the Lord could be such an effective covering to me. Because He was the One tested and proved not only by God, but also by the enemy and all humanity, and because He came forth perfect, bright, and shining; He is the bronze, the burnished bronze; He has the ability, the strength, the qualification, the ground to withstand all attacks. Whenever the enemy meets this perfect One, he flees. Never fight the battle by yourself—this is not your business. The battle is the Lord's.

When I was very young, I heard a story which I can never forget. It has been exceedingly helpful. The father of a little girl had a Christian friend who one day came to see him and have some fellowship. The little girl listened to their fellowship. That gentlemen was greatly troubled. He told the father that he was continually being defeated by the enemy. At length the little girl could not refrain from speaking. She exclaimed, "Sir, I am never defeated by the enemy! You are much bigger than I, but you always lose the battle and I always win the battle!" "Oh!" said the friend, "What is this?" He turned with astonishment to look at her. "Tell me," he said, "how do you win the battle?" "Oh, it's easy," the little girl answered. "When the enemy comes to me and knocks at my door, I ask him, 'Who are you?' He says, 'I am Satan.' Then I say, 'Okay, wait! I'm going to call Jesus!' And I do. Then the enemy says, 'Never mind; I'm going to run away!' And he runs away. This is my way. It's so easy to win the battle."

Whether this story is true or not, I do not know, but of one thing I am sure: if you attempt to fight the battle by yourself, you will surely lose. But whenever you go to the battle with Christ and exercise your faith to apply Him, you will most certainly win. Christ is the tested One, the proved One. He is your covering. The enemy can say nothing to Him and do nothing with Him. Learn to apply Him as your covering.

The Lord has been thoroughly tested. Now He is the One who has been qualified to judge others. He has the bronze; He has the covering.

APPLYING THE IRON

Now, what about the authority, the iron? The Lord said that all authority in heaven and in earth has been given to Him. But this is not the end of the story. The Lord also told us that He has given this authority to us. Brothers and sisters, do you know that you have the right to claim the authority of the Lord? You have something more than power; you have *authority*! Do you know the difference between authority and power?

Let us illustrate. You have an automobile, and with that automobile you have power. Now suppose you meet a policeman on the street, directing traffic with his whistle. He is just a little policeman, but when he stands there and raises his hand, all the cars must stop. What is this? This is authority, the authority of the government. That little policeman represents the government. You must take his orders. It does not matter what kind of car you have or how powerful it is. You must stop! Whether you have a car, a truck, or a bus, it matters not. When he says "Stop!" you stop! The policeman's *power* compared with that of all the cars, or even with one of the cars, is much inferior; in fact, it is almost nil. But he has something which you with your powerful car do not have— that is, authority. When he says "Stop!" everyone must stop! His authority surpasses your power.

Regardless of how strong the enemy is, the most he has is power. We have the authority. We have the authority of the Head of the whole universe. That little policeman represents the city government, but we represent the King of the universe! Brothers and sisters, have you ever enjoyed this authority? I am afraid when trouble comes, you simply forget it and act like a pitiful beggar. You forget that you are representing Christ—*none other than Christ!* The authority committed to Christ has been committed to *you*. The Lord told us that He has given us authority to overcome all the power of the enemy. Oh, what a salvation is this! Oh, may we realize it and experience it! Try to apply the authority given to you by Christ.

That little policeman standing there has the authority to stop all the traffic. But if I go there and say "Stop!" I may very well lose my life. I do not have the ground; I do not have the uniform. Do not think that just because you are a Christian, you can exercise authority over the enemy. You have the authority, but there is a problem. Are you living in Christ? Are you living in the resurrection? That little policeman can stand there today and give all the orders: whatever he binds is bound; whatever he looses is loosed. But if the same person stands there tomorrow, but without his uniform, he can do nothing; no one will follow his directions, and he will be in danger of his life. When he is in uniform, the traffic must obey him; but when he is out of uniform, he is meaningless directing traffic and no match for the cars. You are a Christian, but where are you standing? Where are you living? Where are you walking? Are you walking in Christ, or are you walking in your natural life? If you are in yourself, if you are in your natural life, you have lost the ground, you are out of uniform, and you have no authority.

The apostle Paul in his day cast out many evil spirits (Acts 16:18; 19:12). He addressed the evil spirits and commanded them to leave in the name of the Lord Jesus. But you remember how others, the seven sons of Sceva, attempted to do the same thing in the same name. The evil spirits, instead of leaving, leaped upon them and gave them such an assault that they fled naked and wounded (vv. 13-16). They had no ground; they had no authority. The evil spirits knew Paul and obeyed him, but not these men. The authority depends upon the man.

We must realize from where the iron comes. It comes from the stones. And where are the stones? The stones are in the mountains; the stones are in resurrection. When you are still in the position of a piece of clay, you can never claim the authority. As a natural man of clay, you have no ground, no right; you have no iron in you. But when you are a stone, living in Christ, living in the resurrection, you automatically have the authority. You need not ask for it; you may just claim it and apply it. You can say, "I am living in Christ; I have the authority of the heavens, and I am going to use it!" I tell you, it really works.

The Lord said to us, "Whatever you bind on the earth shall have been bound in heaven, and whatever you loose on the earth shall have been loosed in heaven" (Matt. 18:18). This is authority. But remember, you must be in the resurrection life; you must have the resurrection ground. This is something related to resurrection. Then you have the kingdom, you have the hills. This is how the kingdom comes into being. Because we realize the judgment and the authority of Christ, we can exercise the judgment and the authority of Christ. With us are the mountains, the kingdom, the divine government, the authority of God.

In Deuteronomy 33:25 we are told that the doorbolts of the gates are made of iron and copper. These gates are for our protection, our defense, our safeguard. If we are able to exercise the Lord's authority and the Lord's judgment, we will have the safety and security. Our doors will be bolted with the authority and judgment of the Lord. The most safe and the most secure are those believers who know something regarding the exercise of Christ's authority. They have strength because they have authority, so they have safety and security and therefore rest.

The building of God is always with this kind of Christians. They are not only the material for the building, not only the stones for the house, but the house built together. With this kind of believers is the authority of God, the divine government; therefore, with them is the kingdom of God, the mountains or the hills. We have to grow gradually, of course, from the first stage, through the second, to the third, and to the fourth. We have to learn how to apply Christ to enjoy Him in the first stage as the living water. We must also learn to apply Him in the second stage as the solid food. We must learn to enjoy Christ to such an extent that He will be as sweet and rich to us as milk and honey all the day. Then we will be mature. We will come to the point where we have the ground to claim the authority and the judgment of the Lord.

When we have the authority, there is no need for us to deal with so many things. Even to pray about many matters is not necessary. We have the right to exercise authority over these things. When traffic approaches the policeman, does he need to call the mayor and ask that he do something to stop it? Ridiculous! The policeman is authorized to do this. In exactly the same manner, there is no need for us to call to God for help. We may and we must simply take our ground and exercise our authority.

But, let me repeat, we cannot do this without some degree of spiritual maturity. The apostle Paul undoubtedly had the ground to claim the authority. When a certain problem arose regarding a brother in the church at Corinth and the apostle could not tolerate it, he told them that he judged and delivered that person into the hand of Satan in the name of the Lord Jesus (1 Cor. 5:3-5). He exercised his right; he assumed the authority. If we would do likewise, we like Paul must have the maturity of life.

Oh, brothers and sisters, we must look to the Lord that we may learn day by day how to apply such an all-inclusive

Christ with His unsearchable riches. We must experience Him from the living water all the way to the iron and the copper.

There are many more items of the riches of Christ. I have merely given you some hints in these chapters. We have read the passage in Ezekiel 34:29: "I will raise up for them a planting place of renown." Christ is a plant of renown—we do not know its name. Christ is another special kind of plant. Oh, Christ is exceedingly rich! We can never exhaust Him. There are also other kinds of plants in the Scriptures representing Christ. The second chapter of the Song of Songs speaks of the apple tree. This, however, is not an accurate translation. A more accurate translation indicates that it is a kind of orange tree. Christ is an orange tree. There are so many plants representing Christ and revealing various aspects of His riches for us to experience. Exodus 30 names the plants from which the anointing oil and the incense were composed: myrrh, sweet cinnamon, sweet calamus, and cassia (vv. 23-24), as well as stacte, onycha, galbanum—all sweet spices—with pure frankincense (v. 34). These plants are very meaningful and exceedingly sweet. Oh, the riches! Oh, the inexhaustible riches!

This land is indeed a good land, an exceedingly good land. It is especially good in its unsearchable riches. How rich this piece of land is! It is the type of the all-inclusive Christ. Let us endeavor to experience, to enjoy, and to apply such a glorious, all-inclusive One. May He be gracious to us.

CHAPTER NINE

HOW TO POSSESS THE LAND

(1)

BY THE LAMB, THE MANNA, THE ARK, AND THE TABERNACLE

Ephesians 3:17-18: That Christ may make His home in your hearts through faith, that you, being rooted and grounded in love, may be full of strength to apprehend with all the saints what the breadth and length and height and depth are.

In these two verses several things must be noticed and remembered well. Note the phrase *make His home* in verse 17. It is a big word, a weighty word. In the original tongue, the word for *make His home*, or *dwell*, has the same root as the word for *house* and *home*. We wish to translate that original word in the Greek into "make His home." This conveys a deeper and fuller meaning than "dwell." Christ wants to *make His home* in our hearts, that we may be strong to apprehend. Now notice that it is not just that we may be able to apprehend but that we may "be full of strength" to apprehend. This also is a strong and weighty word. In the Greek it means "to have full power." We could translate the verse in this way: "That you may have full power to apprehend." Now I would call your attention to the word *apprehend*. We are not just to know or understand but to possess something by knowing, to obtain something by understanding—to apprehend. What are we to apprehend? The breadth, the length, the height, and the depth—the spaciousness of Christ, the unlimited dimensions of Christ. Next, we are to apprehend such a Christ *with all the saints*. It is impossible for a single person to apprehend such an unlimited One; it must be with all the saints.

In summary, Christ wants to make His home in our hearts. Then we will have full power to apprehend, to obtain by understanding, the unlimited spaciousness of Christ with all the saints.

> Exodus 33:14-15: He said, My presence shall go with you, and I will give you rest. And he said to Him, If Your presence does not go with us, do not bring us up from here.

The first point here is that the Lord promised Moses that His presence would go with him and the people of Israel. The second point is that the Lord promised Moses to give him rest. The rest which the Lord referred to here is the rest in the good land.

> Deuteronomy 12:10: When you cross over the Jordan and dwell in the land which Jehovah your God is giving you as an inheritance, and when He gives you rest from all your enemies surrounding you so that you dwell securely.

> Deuteronomy 25:19: Therefore when Jehovah your God gives you rest from all your enemies surrounding you, in the land which Jehovah your God is giving you as an inheritance to possess.

By these two verses we see that when the Lord refers to the rest, He is referring to the land. The land is the rest. To possess the land and to dwell there is to be in rest.

> Exodus 40:1-2: Then Jehovah spoke to Moses, saying, On the first day of the first month you shall raise up the tabernacle of the Tent of Meeting.

The Lord commanded Moses to raise up the tabernacle on the first day of the first month. This means an absolutely new beginning.

> Exodus 40:17, 21, 34-35: In the first month in the second year, on the first day of the month, the tabernacle was raised up...And he brought the Ark into the tabernacle and set up the veil for the screen and screened the Ark of the Testimony, as Jehovah had commanded Moses...Then the cloud covered the

Tent of Meeting, and the glory of Jehovah filled the tabernacle. And Moses was not able to enter the Tent of Meeting, because the cloud settled on it and the glory of Jehovah filled the tabernacle. Once the tabernacle was raised up, the glory of the Lord immediately filled it. What is the glory of the Lord? It is the presence of the Lord manifested before the eyes of humanity. Human eyes, the eyes of the children of Israel, beheld the presence of God in His glory at that time.

We have seen something of the goodness, the exceeding goodness, of the land of Canaan, and we have seen how it is the type of the all-inclusive Christ. We have not by any means exhausted all its riches, but I believe we have seen enough to give us a sense of appreciation. Now we must see the way to possess that piece of land. We must see how to enter and enjoy it.

A CORPORATE MATTER

First, to possess this land is not the business of a single person. It is absolutely impossible for anyone as a single individual to do it. We must remember this well. We can never possess the all-inclusive Christ by ourselves as individuals. Absolutely not! Brothers and sisters, let us not dream. Such dreams can never be realized. This is the business of the Body; it is to be apprehended with all saints. Christ is too great; His spaciousness is unlimited and His riches are unsearchable. This principle is firmly established by the Lord: to enter in and take possession of the good land is not for individuals but for a corporate body. The Lord never asked the children of Israel one by one to gradually, singly, and individually cross the Jordan and enter the land. It was never God's mind that one should enter this month, another next month, and still another the following month. This is impossible and contrary to the divine principle. It must be possessed by a corporate body; it must be entered corporately, not individually.

I fear that even while you have been reading these pages, you have been asking, "How can *I* get into this land?" You, as an individual, can never get in. You must be deeply impressed.

This is not the way. If you would enter this land, you must enter as a part of a corporate body.

THE LAMB

At the very beginning, the people of Israel enjoyed the lamb of the passover (Exo. 12), which we know was the type of Christ (1 Cor. 5:7). While they were still in the land of Egypt, they enjoyed Christ. Yet the land of Canaan is also a type of Christ. The lamb is Christ, and the land also is Christ. Seemingly, then, there are two Christs: a smaller Christ and a larger Christ, a Christ as small as the passover lamb and a Christ as great as the land of Canaan. It seems that while we are enjoying this little Christ, a greater Christ is still awaiting us, and we must press on to this goal to enjoy such a One. Is this not true? When I was young, it seemed like this. I had something already, for I had this Christ, but on the other hand, I still had to press on to obtain Him. Then are there two Christs or only one? It seems that I am asking a strange question. Do you have Christ already? I believe you do. Then why are you still endeavoring to obtain Him? If we say we have Him, yet we still must obtain Him; if we say we possess Him, yet He is still ahead of us. If we say we do not have Him, it follows that we can never press on further to obtain Him. These questions touch deeply the issue of these messages.

We need to realize that first of all we must enjoy Christ as a little lamb. Christ is the lamb for our redemption. We must firstly be redeemed by Him before we can ever obtain Him as the all-inclusive One. We must receive Him as the lamb of the passover. Thus, we are starting in this chapter from the first part of the book of Exodus. This is the place where we must begin in order to get into the land of Canaan. We must have the passover; we must experience Christ as the Lamb of God. *Behold, the Lamb of God* is at the beginning of John's Gospel (1:29), but at the close of the book Christ is the unlimited One to be possessed by His disciples. At the beginning Christ is the lamb introduced to the people by John the Baptist, but at the end Christ is One who is unlimited by space and time. Nothing can limit that resurrected One, yet He is for our enjoyment. We must experience Christ as the limited lamb; then we may press on to obtain Him as the unlimited Christ.

Actually, in the passover we not only have the lamb but also the unleavened bread and the bitter herbs (Exo. 12:8). Here again we have two kinds of lives. The lamb is of the animal life, and the unleavened bread and bitter herbs are of the vegetable life. At the moment you were saved, whether you were aware of it or not, you experienced Christ as two kinds of lives: you experienced Him as the redeeming lamb as well as the generating and multiplying life. Have you ever noticed this? Then allow me to point out something else. (This matter of the good land can never be exhausted. Another book could be filled with messages upon this subject with nothing repeated.) In John 6 the Lord Jesus combined these two lives into one. He said, "I am the bread of life" (v. 35). What is bread? It is something of wheat or barley, something of the vegetable life. But when the Lord made such a statement, the people could not understand it. Then He declared, "He who eats My flesh and drinks My blood has eternal life...For My flesh is true food, and My blood is true drink" (vv. 54-55). In other words, the bread of life is His flesh. The bread is the vegetable life, and the flesh is the animal life, and in this chapter the Lord Himself binds these two together.

Therefore, brothers and sisters, we must begin by enjoying Christ as the redeeming lamb with the generating power, the multiplying strength. We must take the lamb of the passover with the unleavened bread and the bitter herbs.

THE MANNA

Following the passover, our next experience of Christ is the manna. After we enjoy Him as the lamb, we go on to enjoy Him as our daily food. Is manna something of the vegetable life or of the animal life? Let us look at the Scripture:

> Numbers 11:7-9: Now the manna was like corian-
> der seed, and its appearance like the appearance of
> bdellium. The people went about and gathered it
> and ground it between two millstones or beat it in a
> mortar; then they boiled it in pots and made cakes

of it; and its taste was like the taste of cakes baked
in oil. And when the dew fell on the camp at night,
the manna would fall with it.

Exodus 16:31: The house of Israel called its name
manna, and it was like coriander seed, white; and
its taste was like wafers made with honey.

We have read here that manna is like some sort of seed, and
its taste is like fresh oil and honey. So here again two lives
are mingled together. Notice also at this point that the
appearance of manna is like bdellium. The proper meaning of
bdellium is pearl. In Revelation 21 we see that pearl is one
of the constituents of God's building. Therefore, manna, as
pearl, typifies something transformed as material for the
building of God. Bdellium is the very word used in Genesis 2.
In that passage the tree of life is introduced and then a river
in whose flow are several precious materials, one of which is
bdellium. This means that when we take the tree of life and
drink the water of life, the pearl, the transformed material for
God's building, will be produced.

Manna then is a substance with all these natures: the
nature of the vegetable life, the nature of the animal life, and
the nature of the transformed life. We must enjoy this aspect
of Christ. We must enjoy Him as the lamb of the passover
with the unleavened bread and bitter herbs, and we must continue on to enjoy Him as the manna, including the vegetable
life, the animal life, and the transformed nature. By partak-
ing of Christ as our daily manna, we may be transformed into
material for the building of God.

But is this sufficient? No, there is something more. The
way to get into the land starts from the twelfth chapter of
Exodus and continues on to the last chapter of Joshua. We
must read all these parts thoroughly and understand them
clearly; then we will have the way to possess the land.

THE ARK

To enjoy Christ, starting from the lamb of the passover
and continuing day by day with the manna from heaven, is
just the beginning. We must go on to experience Him as the
Ark, the Ark embodied and covered with the tabernacle (Exo.

25:10-22). What is the Ark? The Ark is the testimony of God. The testimony of God is simply the manifestation of God, the expression of God. In the Ark were the tablets with the Ten Commandments. What are the Ten Commandments?

The impression most Christians have concerning the Ten Commandments is that they are simply the strict demands of God. You should do this and you should do that; you should not do this and you should not do that. This is the impression imparted to us by general Christian teaching. But what is the essential meaning of the Ten Commandments? Apparently they are laws, but the main significance is not that they are laws; that is secondary. The primary significance is that they are the expression of God. The Ten Commandments are the manifestation of God.

What kind of God is God? We may know by the Ten Commandments. You have never seen God, but here are "ten words" (Exo. 34:28, footnote) which give you a description of Him. The first feature is that God is jealous. God wants everything; He will never let anyone rival with Him. He is a jealous God. The second is that He is a holy God. Then there are other features: He is a God of love, He is a righteous God, He is a faithful God, etc. Thus, the Ten Commandments are the description, the expression, the manifestation of the hidden God. They give you an impression of the invisible God and show you what kind of God He is. He is a jealous God; He is a holy God; He is a God of love; He is a righteous God; He is a faithful God. By these Ten Commandments you may discern His nature. Do not pay too much attention to these Ten Commandments as laws. That is secondary. The primary significance, we must realize, is the description, the expression, the testimony of the glorious yet invisible God.

These Ten Commandments were put into the Ark. This signifies that God put Himself into Christ. The Ten Commandments are the testimony of God, and the Ark of the Testimony is Christ. Therefore, the fullness of God dwells in Christ.

The Ark is clearly the type of Christ with two natures. It was made of wood overlaid with gold. Wood is the human nature, and gold is the divine nature. It is a picture of Christ in the flesh mingled with the divine nature. He has the nature of man, and at the same time He has the nature of God—the human nature and the divine. He is the Ark, but within Him is God Himself. Just as the Ten Commandments were put into the Ark, so all that God is was put into Christ. Just as the Ark was called "the Ark of the Testimony," so Christ is the manifestation and testimony of God. This is something more, you see, than the lamb of the passover and the daily manna. This is something solid, perfect, and full. This is the manifestation of God, the expression of God, the testimony of God. By the lamb of the passover, can you realize what God is like? Yes, perhaps you may see a little. By the daily manna, can you be impressed with the nature of God? It is rather difficult. I do not say that you can see nothing, but that you cannot see much. Now come to the Ark. Consider it. Read it. Immediately you know something about God. God is jealous; God is love; God is holy; God is righteous; God is faithful. By the Ark you can immediately realize what the hidden God is like.

But I wish to ask, Can you eat the Ark? Can you drink the Ark? You cannot; but this is another aspect of Christ, a fuller aspect of Christ. Christ is the expression, the manifestation, the testimony of the invisible God. As we enjoy Christ as the lamb of the passover and as our daily manna, we must also have this Christ, this larger Christ (if you would allow me to use this word), as our center. We must have the Ark of the Testimony, the Christ who is the expression, the manifestation, and the testimony of God as our very center. This is indeed more. We must not only have the lamb as our Redeemer and not only the daily manna as our food but also the Ark of the Testimony as our center.

Brothers and sisters, permit me to repeat. I fear that some of you may not be able to follow. Are you enjoying Christ day by day as your daily manna? That is good, but that is not sufficient. We must have Him as our center. What is the center? The center is the expression, the manifestation, the testimony of God. Do we have such a center among us? Is this really the center of our meeting, our church life? When people come to us, can they realize that in our midst is the expression of God? If people come to us and just realize that we are those

who are redeemed, that we are those who enjoy Christ as the
lamb, it is entirely inadequate. If they just realize that we are
those who feed on Christ day by day as the daily manna, even
this misses the mark. We must be able to give them the
impression that among us, in the midst of us, is the manifestation of the jealous God, the God of love, the God of holiness,
the God of righteousness, the God of faithfulness. Do we have
such a center among us or not? When people come to us, do
they realize that here is the manifestation, the expression,
the definition, the explanation, of God? Do they realize that
we are the testimony of God, that we are testifying from the
reality of our experience of Christ that God is a jealous God, a
holy God, a God of love, a righteous God, and a faithful God?
We must have this testimony as our center.

You see, it is not such a simple matter to possess the land.
Do you think that immediately after enjoying the lamb and
crossing the Red Sea we can enter the land? No. After Exodus 12, 13, and 14, after the passover and the crossing of the
Red Sea, there are many more experiences to be gained. The
remainder of Exodus and all of Leviticus, Numbers, Deuteronomy, and Joshua still lie before us. There are many more
things to be dealt with, many more things to experience, many
more things to be possessed, before we can get into the land.

We must see the full meaning of the Ark. There is undoubtedly the aspect of the commandments as laws—we cannot
deal with that aspect here. But more important than that, the
Ten Commandments are the definition, the explanation, the
interpretation, of the invisible God. And this interpretation,
this explanation, is in Jesus Christ, that God-man, that incarnate One with the divine and human natures. He is the
explanation of God; He is the manifestation of God; He is God
Himself. This is the One who must be our center. He is the
expression, the testimony of God, and we should have Him as
our testimony. We should be testifying nothing else but God
manifested in Christ.

THE TABERNACLE

This Ark is embodied within the tabernacle. The Ten Commandments are embodied in the Ark, and the Ark is embodied

within the tabernacle (Exo. 40:20-21). What then is the tabernacle? The tabernacle is the enlargement of the Ark, the increase of the Ark. The Ark was made with wood overlaid with gold, and the major part of the tabernacle was composed of the same materials—wood overlaid with gold (Exo. 26:15-30). The tabernacle, therefore, is the enlargement of the Ark. In other words, the Ark enlarged becomes the tabernacle. The tabernacle is made in the same shape and with the same materials, and it is constituted with and contains within it more of Christ.

Let us see something more of Christ in the tabernacle. We read that there were four layers of covering over it (Exo. 26:1-14). This means that Christ became one of the creatures, since four is the number signifying the creatures. What are these four layers of different kinds of coverings? The outermost one is seal skin, a strong protection against the wind, the rain, and the heat of the sun. Under the seal skin is the rams' skin dyed red, signifying that Christ died and shed His blood for our sins, and under that is the covering of goats' hair, signifying that Christ was made sin for us. The innermost covering is of linen, so beautiful, so fine, so full of glory, with the cherubim embroidered upon it. All these coverings are full of meaning and require much explanation. They all relate to Christ.

From within, you see His glory. Oh, Christ is so glorious from within! From without, you see His lowliness, His humility, His simplicity; you see His strength and His enduring power, but there is no beauty. This is Jesus, despised by others, a lowly man. But within He is the glorious Christ.

Praise the Lord, we are covered with such a Christ! According to the dimensions of the tabernacle, ten curtains were required to form the covering. The innermost covering of fine linen, therefore, was made of ten curtains. But the covering of goats' hair was formed of eleven curtains. It was not five plus five, but five plus six, and six is not a good number. Six refers to man and involves sin. Thus, it signifies that Christ was made sin for us. The innermost layer is the glorious Christ; the second is the Christ who was made sin for us; the third is the Christ who died, shedding His blood; and the fourth, the outermost covering, is the Christ who humbled Himself to become a lowly man. This Christ, this fourfold Christ, covers us. What a covering, what a protection, what a safeguard!

In this tabernacle, Christ is joined with so many boards. We are the wooden boards, the human members: you are one board, and I am another. The Ark is embodied in such a tabernacle, which is Christ joined with us and uniting us all in the divine nature just as all the boards were united in the gold. There were at least forty-eight boards, all overlaid with gold, and joined together with golden rings and bars (Exo. 26:26-29). If we were to remove the gold, all forty-eight boards would fall apart; not one would be joined to another. We are not joined in the flesh, nor could we ever be joined in such a way. It is the divine nature that joins us. The gold is the joint; the gold is the unity among us. Without the gold, we will fall to pieces. I will not agree with you, and you will not agree with me. But, praise the Lord, the gold covers you, and the gold covers me. There are some golden rings on you, and there is a golden bar on me. It is impossible for us to be separated. Even if you like to run away, you cannot. You are bound. You and I are bound together and can never be separated. We are not bound by our natural dispositions—naturally speaking, I may never be able to get along with you. And even if we are naturally compatible, that is not a true or stable union. But, praise the Lord, we are bound in a real and indissoluble union by something divine, by the very nature of God Himself. We are not only bound by the gold, but we are covered by the gold, we are safeguarded by the gold. The gold is God Himself.

One day in my room I said to myself, "How unfortunate you are! You have been captured by the divine nature, and you can't escape. You may try, but you can never get out of this team of gold!" This is the unity. Brothers and sisters, there must be such a unity among us. Then we will be strengthened and qualified to enter the land. If we can escape from each other, if we can be separated from one another, there is no way for us to go into the good land. We must have this tabernacle, this embodiment of the Ark. We must be bound together in this divine nature as the tabernacle to the

Ark. The Ark, which is Christ, is within as our center, and we are the enlargement of this Christ as the tabernacle embodying the Ark.

We have seen how we must enjoy Christ as the lamb of the passover, as the daily manna, and as the Ark embodied within the tabernacle. All these are our qualifications to enter the land.

Chapter Ten

HOW TO POSSESS THE LAND

(2)

BY THE OFFERINGS AND THE PRIESTHOOD

Scripture Reading: Lev. 1:1-3; 2:1; 3:1; 4:2, 3; 5:5, 6; 8:1-13; Exo. 40:17, 21

We have begun to see the way to enter the land and take possession of the all-inclusive Christ. We have pointed out that if we would possess such a One, we must begin by enjoying Him little by little. The people of Israel began to enjoy the types of Christ with the lamb of the passover—that is the place where we all must start. Then they moved on to enjoy Him as the heavenly manna, and then as the rock flowing with the living water. All these are types of Christ, but they are elementary types; they are not so deep and rich. To our realization they may be quite sufficient, but we must realize that they are just the start.

We have seen the Ark and the testimony of God within it. The Ark is another type of Christ, one which is much more solid and full. If you compare the Ark with the lamb, the manna, or the rock flowing with living water, you can see what an improvement there is. Much more of Christ is manifested by the Ark. In the lamb of the passover, you may realize Christ only as the redeeming One, the One who died on the cross, shedding His blood for our sins. The manna is an improvement and really a good experience. In it you taste the vegetable life and the animal life, and at the same time you touch something of the pearl as the transformed material for God's building. These experiences are indeed good, but they

are no match for the Ark. The experience of the Ark is much
more solid, and its content incomparably more full. You can
read something within it. There is something written about
God Himself. By the content of the Ark, you may know the
very nature of God.

With the Ark is its embodiment, its increase, and enlargement—the tabernacle. The tabernacle is the enlargement and
expression of Christ, for the major part of the tabernacle is
of exactly the same nature as that of the Ark. The Ark was
constructed with wood overlaid with gold, and the tabernacle
was made in the same way with the same materials. But how
may we realize that the tabernacle is the enlargement and
expression of Christ as His Body, the church? Because it was
composed of forty-eight wooden boards. It was constituted of
so many boards, typifying the members of the Body. In the
church, many members are built together by being overlaid
and bound together with the divine gold. They are one in the
gold. They are covered with gold and joined one to another in
the golden rings and bars. If they are out of the gold, they fall
to pieces and are alienated from each other. They are pieces
in the human nature, but in the divine nature, in the Triune
God, they are one. Furthermore, they are all covered by the
fourfold Christ, just as the tabernacle was covered with the
four layers of curtains. The church, which is the enlargement
of Christ, the expression of Christ, is under such a covering.
All these forty-eight boards were standing on silver sockets
or bases, meaning that they are based on the redemption of
Christ. The redemption of Christ is the basis upon which they
stand to be overlaid and bound together with the divine gold
and covered over with the fourfold Christ. This is the church,
the increase and expression of Christ.

We can realize that this is much more than the lamb of
the passover, the manna, and the rock flowing with the living stream. Here is something solid. Here is Christ with the
testimony of God within and His enlargement as the real
expression of Himself without. This Christ is the center of
those who are going on to possess the land. If we would take
possession of the all-inclusive Christ, we must have such a
Christ as our center, a Christ with the testimony in Himself,

a Christ who is the manifestation and the explanation of God. And we must be the enlargement of this Christ, the tabernacle for this Christ, the expression of this Christ. We should have such a center, and we should be such an enlargement. This is the way for us to possess the land. This does not mean that we have a tremendous amount of the experiences of Christ but that our enjoyment of Him is increasing and enlarging all the time.

We start by enjoying a lamb. We must say a *little* lamb. It is perfect and complete, but it is little. Then we learn to enjoy Christ daily as the manna, as our food supply, and as the rock flowing with the living stream. Christ becomes more to us. Then we begin to experience Christ as the testimony of God, the manifestation and explanation of God. Christ is being formed in us to a fuller extent and in a more solid way. When people come to us, they realize that this is our center; they read the nature of God Himself. We become Christ's enlargement, His fullness, His Body. This should be our experience and our testimony.

THE TABERNACLE FILLED WITH GLORY

When we have the Ark as our center and we are built together as the tabernacle to embody this Ark, then the glory of God comes down and fills the tabernacle. It is not until we have this testimony, until we experience Christ as the Ark, as the manifestation of God, and until we are the expression of the Ark, the enlargement of Christ, that we are filled with the glory of God. We should experience Christ in such a way. He is the expression of God, and we must be the expression of Him. Then the glory of God will fill us. We may be sure that whenever we reach this point, it matters not when or how we meet, formally or informally, the very glory of God will be with us. What is glory? As we have already mentioned, it is the presence of God realized by human sense. When you can sense the presence of God, that is glory. Where is this glory? It is where the Ark is the center and where the tabernacle is built up as the enlargement and embodiment of it.

The glory of God may be illustrated by an electric light bulb. The bulb is a vessel to display the glory of the electricity.

When not connected to electricity, it has no glory and is rather meaningless. But when everything is in order and the electricity is switched on, the glory fills the bulb. Everyone can see it. Everyone can recognize it and sense the glory.

When the point is reached where we have such a Christ as the manifestation of God and we are the expression of such a Christ, the glory of God will fill us whenever we come together. People can sense it. They can sense the very expression of God because God is glorified among us. Not until we attain this stage is there such reality. When we take Christ as the passover lamb, there is not such an expression of glory. Even when we enjoy Him as the daily manna and as the rock flowing with the living stream, the shekinah glory is missing. It is not until one day the Ark is put into the tabernacle and the tabernacle is raised up upon the silver sockets and covered with the fourfold covering that the glory of God descends.

This is a clear picture of the real expression of Christ. The real expression of Christ is the enlargement of Christ Himself. It is Christ as the manifestation of God mingled with us. It is neither the little passover lamb, nor even Christ as the daily manna and the rock, but Christ, the manifestation of God among us as the center, mingled with us, enlarged within us, and increased among us. Everyone of us has been saturated with the nature of Christ and built up together in Him. Christ is of two natures, the human and the divine, and we are the same: we are of the human nature but covered with the divine. He is the God-man, and we are the God-men. He is the Ark made of wood covered with gold, and we are the boards made of wood covered with gold. In number we are different, but in nature we are exactly the same. Christ is the manifestation of God, and all these boards combined together as one in the gold are the expression of Christ. When this point is reached, the God of glory comes down and fills us. This is the testimony. We are testifying nothing but this Christ who is the manifestation of God and who has been enlarged through us, thereby filling us with the glory of God.

I can relate numerous stories to illustrate this point. Many times I have experienced such a glory, a wonderful glory.

Many times when I have been with a group of believers who have come to such a stage, the glory has come down. Everyone knows it. When we experience Christ not just as the passover lamb and the manna, but together in this fuller and solid way, we always have the glory among us.

THE OFFERINGS

But this is not all. This is not the end of the story. Even if we have this, we are still not qualified to enter that good land. We must have something more. We started with Exodus 12 by enjoying Christ as the redeeming lamb; we have also seen what it means to go on and enjoy Him as the daily manna and as the rock flowing with the living water; and we have seen the enjoyment of Christ as the Ark, as the manifestation of the living God, and us as the expression, the enlargement of this Christ, so that the glory of God fills us. We have finished the book of Exodus, and we come now to the next book, Leviticus.

After the tabernacle is reared up, we must deal next with the offerings. How rich Christ is to us in all the various offerings! Perhaps you are saying, "Oh, we have seen so much of Christ already; it is sufficient!" But, no, we must go on. There is much more. The tabernacle is reared up, but how may we get in contact with this tabernacle? Here is the testimony, here is the manifestation of God, here is the expression of Christ, but how can we contact these? We cannot go on to contact this testimony in ourselves. Never. There is an entrance, but the only proper way for us to approach this entrance and contact the tabernacle is by the offerings. To contact the tabernacle without the offerings means immediate death. When we come to contact this tabernacle, we must have some offerings. Oh, Christ is so rich! On one hand, He is the manifestation of God, and on the other hand, He is the way by which we can contact this God: He is the offerings. He is the very means by which we may contact the manifestation of God, which is Himself. He is everything.

What are the offerings? There are five: the burnt offering, the meal offering, the peace offering, the sin offering, and the trespass offering. They are all Christ. Whenever we would deal with the testimony, whenever we would contact the expression of Christ, we must offer Christ once more, we must apply Christ once more. Sometimes we need to apply Him as the trespass offering, sometimes as the sin offering, sometimes as the meal offering, sometimes as the peace offering, and sometimes even more as the burnt offering.

When should we apply Christ as the trespass offering? It is quite clear. Let me illustrate. Suppose we are having a meeting and you are coming to the meeting; you are coming to contact the tabernacle with Christ as its center. But in your heart you have the registration that you have done something wrong. Perhaps you have been wrong with one of your brothers. Yes, you saw him today and even smiled at him, but that kind of smile was an expression of hatred. When you come to contact the tabernacle and the testimony, the Holy Spirit causes you to sense your trespass. You have sinned; you have trespassed. The Lord has told you to love your brother, but you have loved him in a false way; you have smiled at him with hatred. Thus, you must apply Christ as the trespass offering.

Many times you can tell the truth, but with a lie. In other words, you lie with the truth. Sometimes I ask a brother concerning the state of another brother. He replies that the brother is quite well, but by the tone and the sense of the spirit, I can detect that on one hand he is telling the truth, but on the other hand it is a lie. I may ask if you love a certain brother, and you may reply that by the grace of God you do. If so, I know you do not love him. I may ask if you are a good brother, and you may answer that you are not so good. It seems that you are being humble and honest. But in your heart you are saying that you are the best brother. Oh, brothers and sisters, we are trespassing all the time!

How selfish we are! We are selfish to such an extent that when we come to the meeting we choose the best seat. Here in America you have separate seats, so you cannot take advantage of others, but in Formosa they have long benches. All the benches are of sufficient length to seat four persons during the usual meetings. But when they have a conference, they ask the brothers and sisters to sit as closely as possible in order to make the bench available for five. Some, however, knowing this, spread out and occupy one fourth of the bench, compelling others to take less. What kind of way is this to contact the tabernacle and testimony of the Lord? How sinful we are! How much we need to apply the Lord as our trespass offering!

Brothers and sisters, I believe that if we are faithful and honest before the Lord, when we come to contact this tabernacle, this testimony, His Spirit will cause us to sense all our sinfulness and all our trespasses. We will sense what we have done, and we will say, "O Lord, forgive me. Cleanse me. You have died on the cross as my Redeemer; so once more I apply you as my trespass offering." Oh, it is wonderful! Whenever we apply Christ in such a way, we immediately sense that we have been forgiven and cleansed. We are at peace in our conscience. We have good fellowship with the Lord and with the Body. This is the application of Christ as our trespass offering. Do you have this kind of experience?

Every time, without one exception, when I am preparing to minister, I must ask the Lord to cleanse me once more. Otherwise, because of the condemnation in my conscience, I will not have the anointing and will not be able to minister in a living way. I must apply Christ every time as my trespass offering so that my conscience will be pure and I will be at peace. Then I have the boldness to claim the anointing of God. Where the blood cleanses, there the anointing will come. The anointing of the ointment always follows the cleansing of the blood. We have the ground of the blood to claim the anointing, the working of the Holy Spirit, so that we can minister in a living way. When I apply Christ as my trespass offering, it matters not how much I have trespassed. Praise the Lord, I am forgiven and cleansed. Whenever I come to minister, whenever I come to serve, and even when I contact some brothers, I have to say, "Lord, forgive me and cleanse me once more. I apply You as my trespass offering."

Sometimes it seems that we have not trespassed. By the protection of the Lord, we have been kept through the entire day in His presence without any trespasses. It is possible. We do not sense that we have trespassed, but we have a deeper feeling. It is quite strange. When we are saying, "Lord, I praise You, You have kept me through the whole day; by Your protection I have not trespassed," we have a deeper feeling that within us is something sinful. We sense that deeply within is something which is more sinful than trespasses. It is Sin, capitalized Sin. It is the sinful *nature*. Though we have been saved and have peace with God and with one another, yet within us is a sinful nature. This is the Sin which is dealt with so extensively in Romans 5, 6, 7, and 8. Sin dwells within me. I am not speaking of sins, but Sin—capitalized, singular Sin. I hate to do what I do. It is not I that do it, but Sin which dwells in me. There is an evil, but powerful, living matter within me called Sin. It can conquer me; it can defeat me; it can cause me to do things which I detest. It is a living nature; it is the nature of the evil one. For this there is an offering— the sin offering.

One day I was reading in the newspaper concerning a man who robbed a bank. I said, "O Lord, I thank You that by Your mercy and grace I have never done such a thing; I have never robbed others." But deeply within me was a sense that I should not say this, for the very robbing element is in me. True, I have not had the robbing *act,* but I have the robbing *nature.* On one hand, I can say, "Lord, I thank You that by Your protection I have not engaged in the act of robbing others." But on the other hand, I must say, "Lord, I have a sinful nature, a robbing nature, but You are my sin offering. Though I have no trespasses outwardly, yet I have a sinful nature inwardly. Though I do not need to apply You now as my trespass offering, yet I still need You as my sin offering."

Brothers and sisters, whenever we as fallen creatures come to contact the testimony of the Lord, we must at least apply Christ as the sin offering. In the Scriptures we see that the children of Israel had to offer the sin offering to contact the Lord. It does not matter how good you feel you are. You must realize that since you are still in the sinful nature, you must still apply Christ as the sin offering.

Praise the Lord that He is also the peace offering. Day by day and even moment by moment, as we enjoy Him as our trespass offering and our sin offering, we also enjoy Him as our peace offering. Through Him and in Him we have peace with God and we have peace with our brothers and sisters. Christ Himself is our peace. We enjoy Him as our peace with God and our peace with men. He is so sweet, He is so satisfying; everyone of us may enjoy Him in the presence of God and enjoy Him together with God. This is Christ as the peace offering.

Sometimes we must apply Christ as the meal offering. Many times after we have applied and experienced Him as the trespass offering and as the sin offering, we will immediately apply Him as the meal offering. We simply enjoy Christ. We enjoy His life upon earth—how He was so perfect, so fine, so pure, and so spiritual! We enjoy Him as such a One. We say, "Lord, how we enjoy You as the meal offering to God." This is the way to offer Christ as the meal offering.

We must also apply Christ many times as the burnt offering. We have to say, "O Lord, I realize how You have wholly offered Yourself to God as a sacrifice to do His will, to satisfy Him, to have a life absolutely for God. I enjoy You as such a One." Many times at the Lord's table we have this sort of experience. We apply Christ as the meal offering and as the burnt offering. We see that wondrous life of the Lord when He was here. We see Him when He was twelve years of age. We see Him as a carpenter in that poor family in Nazareth. We see how He acted when He came forth in His ministry for God, how He conducted Himself before others and how He treated them so kindly, so gently, so humbly, and so holily. We apply Him as our enjoyment, as our meal offering and as our burnt offering for God's satisfaction. We can say to the Lord, "You lived on this earth absolutely for God. You are the burnt offering. I apply You as my enjoyment and God's satisfaction, not only here at Your table but during the day. Sometimes in the morning and sometimes in the evening, I enjoy You as the meal offering and the burnt offering."

Oh, praise the Lord that He is all these offerings for us to enjoy! The more you and I apply Christ as the trespass offering, as the sin offering, as the peace offering, as the meal offering, and as the burnt offering, the more we feel that we are in the tabernacle. The more we apply Christ in such a way, the more we feel we are in the glorious presence of God. This is not just a doctrine, but something so real. It can be proved; it can be experienced. If we do not have such experiences, something is wrong with us.

Now you see how much of Christ we have to experience. We have to experience Him as the lamb of the passover, as the manna, as the rock, as the Ark with the tabernacle, and as all the offerings—trespass, sin, peace, meal, and burnt. We have to experience Christ and apply Christ hour by hour, instance by instance, in such a way that we will be qualified, enabled, and strengthened to go on and take possession of the all-inclusive Christ. Gaining possession of this good land does not take place suddenly or instantaneously. It is a gradual process. First we must enjoy Him as the lamb; then we must enjoy Him as the manna, as the rock, as the Ark with the tabernacle; and then day by day and instance after instance we must enjoy Him as all the various kinds of offerings. Then we will be qualified and matured to gain possession of that all-inclusive land. But there is more to follow.

THE PRIESTHOOD

Immediately after the offerings in the first part of Leviticus, we are introduced to the priesthood. Aaron and his sons were all adorned and qualified to serve as priests to God. We must have this; we must have Christ as our Aaron, Christ as our high priest, and all of us must be His sons, the priests to serve the Lord. This is something more to enjoy, something more to experience and apply. When you come to the meeting to enjoy the Lord, do you serve, do you function, do you minister? Perhaps you will answer, "Brother, I am not a minister; I don't minister. You are the minister." But if you tell me that you are not a minister, I will tell you that I am not a minister either. I am what you are. You are a brother, and I am a brother too. But, brothers and sisters, you must realize that you have to minister. We all have to minister. What should you minister? You know. If you are sincere and faithful to the Lord, you will know what you have to minister. You are a priest.

If you are not serving as priests, you can never take possession of the all-inclusive Christ. If you would enter into that good land, you must be a priest. There must be a priesthood among the Lord's children before the entrance into the land will be available. Perhaps you will say that many of the children of Israel were not priests. But you do recognize that they were all profited by the priesthood. In any case, there was a priesthood among them, and there must also be a priesthood among us.

What is a priest? Please do not consider that the priests among God's children today are those so-called ministers, pastors, preachers, etc. I am afraid that many of them are not genuine priests. Who are the priests today? They are those who are living in Christ and by Christ to manifest Christ. It does not matter what you do or what your job is. You may be a school teacher, a businessman, a doctor, a nurse, a student, or a housewife. The essential and basic thing is that you live in Christ, walk in Christ, enjoy Christ, experience Christ, and apply Christ to all your life. This makes you a priest. Consider the sons of Aaron when they were brought to Moses. What did Moses do? He removed their clothes and put upon them the priestly robes. What are the priestly robes? They are the manifestation of Christ. Christ manifested upon you is the robe of the priest. What the priests eat represents Christ, what they wear represents Christ, and all their living represents Christ. To be a priest you must live in Christ and serve with Christ. When you teach in school, you teach in Christ; when you do business, you do business in Christ; when you take care of your home, you do it in Christ. You are in the robe of a priest.

A sister recently came to us from a distant city. She sent us a telegram, indicating her time of arrival and her flight number, but none of us knew her or had ever met her before. To further complicate the situation, it was a holiday season and the airport was crowded with travelers. The brothers were very much concerned and talked with me, saying, "Brother, how will we be able to recognize this sister? How will she know us?" "Be at peace," I said, "there will be some signs; we will know her." When the plane arrived and the passengers began to deplane, we were waiting at the entrance. Several ladies went by, and then several more. As we watched them pass, I said to one of the brothers, "This is not the one. This is not her. No, not that one. No... No..." Then another one was coming, and I said to the brother, "This is her; this one must be her. Go ahead and speak to her." And this very one was smiling at us. She was the right one. I recognized her from her "priestly robe."

About thirty years ago, another sister came to us in north China by boat from Shanghai. The ship could not dock at the pier; so many small ferries brought the guests to shore. A multitude of friends and relatives were there, shouting and welcoming this one and that one. But we had never seen this sister; we did not know her. We looked at this one, and we looked at that one. We scanned and searched every ferry that arrived, but we could not distinguish anyone as the sister. Finally, another ferry came carrying a lady, and when she came within eyesight, we all said it was her. We were right. How could we tell? Just by a certain kind of manifestation. I cannot explain the signs, but I can realize them, I can sense them.

There are many stories like this. If you are a priest, there is something about you which is not ordinary; you have distinct and distinguishing characteristics. You are equipped with Christ, you are adorned with Christ; Christ is your robe. You must experience Christ in such a way; then you will be a priest. Whatever you handle, you will handle with Christ; whatever you do, you will do with Christ. You will manifest Christ. If you are a sister and you are handling Christ all the day, think how much you will be able to minister to the Lord. You will help people to know Christ; you will minister Christ to your family. When you come to the meetings, you will be able to minister many things. Whether you clean or arrange the seats or kneel down with two or three other sisters to pray for the meeting, it is all a ministry, a ministry fulfilled in Christ, with Christ, and by Christ. Perhaps you will prepare some food for guests who will come for special meetings. That is also a ministry which must be filled with the Spirit. In Acts we are told that those who served the tables must be filled with the Spirit. It is not an easy matter to handle the preparation of food. It is an excellent opportunity to apply Christ and minister Christ.

There are many ministries for the priests to perform. You can come and sit here in the meeting, and although you may not be taking an active part openly in the meeting, yet you may have a powerful and prevailing ministry every moment. In Shanghai, during the period of 1946 through 1948, I delivered the greater part of the messages. I can tell you that whenever I was releasing a message, some brothers and sisters—not a small number, perhaps one or two hundred—were sitting there ministering. They were ministering by the spirit, by a praying spirit, by a receiving spirit. They were sitting there to draw out my message by their spirit. That was their ministry, and it was most effective and valuable. There were hundreds of people crowded into that meeting place, but they were my backers, my supporters. They were so one with me. Without them I could not minister in such a living and released way.

One time we arranged some special meetings to preach the gospel to the unbelievers. All the brothers and sisters considered it best to reserve the seats for their unsaved friends; so they withdrew to another room. Hence, all the hall, especially in the front, was filled with unbelievers. When I arose to minister, I looked around and received a real shock. Not one backer, not one supporter was there. I had to fight the battle all by myself. The weight of all those unbelievers, those sons of the devil, was exceedingly heavy. They crowded around me, and their sins rose against me. The next day I told the brothers and sisters, "No, no, you must never do that! At least two hundred of you must stay to support me. I cannot fight with hundreds of people singled-handed. You must come back. You must sit with all the people to pray and receive."

With such a supporting spirit, what boldness and authority there is! Everyone is subdued, not by me, but by the Body, by the priesthood. On the day of Pentecost, Peter did not stand alone, but he stood with the eleven. See his boldness. See his authority. See the prevailing results.

One year in Taiwan we had a large conference with more than two thousand in attendance. As I faced it, a great burden was upon me. I was deeply burdened. I said to the elders, "You all have to come with me to the platform." Thus, when we arrived at the meetings, they all came up to the platform, and while I stood to deliver the messages, there was a resounding Amen! Amen! They supported me; they backed me. I had much boldness, and the entire congregation was subdued. The fear of the Lord and the love of the Lord are stirred up by this kind of atmosphere. This is the ministry. Brothers and sisters, we can never fool the enemy, we can never fool our conscience, and we can never fool the Lord. If those elders on the platform were not priests, if they were worldly people, it would have been impossible for them to say Amen in such a way. There would be no peace in their conscience. They might have said Amen softly and weakly, but that is meaningless; there is no support in that. But they were serving the Lord in Christ; they were living in Christ, with Christ, and by Christ. Therefore, they had great boldness. When the occasion arose that a brother must minister, they could say, "Let us go with him to the platform as an army." Not just one brother was ministering but a team, an army. When he spoke, they all said Amen with a strong spirit and drove the enemy away. There was no room for the enemy, and the whole meeting with the entire congregation was conquered and captured by the Lord. If you have had such an experience or have been in such a meeting, you can testify to the reality of this.

Brothers and sisters, this is the real ministry. It all depends on how much you live in Christ, walk in Christ, and take Christ as your food, your clothing, and your everything.

Now we have finished Leviticus. How many items of Christ we have to experience! How rich, how wonderfully rich He is! We must experience Him more and more. Now we not only have the Ark with the tabernacle but the offerings and the priesthood. We are much more qualified to enter the land, but we must not be proud. We have to practice all these things day by day and experience them in reality. By enjoying Christ as the lamb, the passover feast, the daily manna, the rock with the living water, the Ark with the tabernacle, all the various offerings, and all the equipment and supply of the real priesthood, we are qualified to enter that good land.

CHAPTER ELEVEN

HOW TO POSSESS THE LAND

(3)

BY THE GOVERNING PRINCIPLES

Scripture Reading: Exo. 40:36-38; Lev. 8:7, 8, 10-12, 30; 20:26; 26:46

Before going on to Numbers, we must see something more in the two books of Exodus and Leviticus. We have seen that the way to enter the good land is by enjoying Christ step by step in an ever increasing measure, starting from the lamb of the passover. But there is something in our experience which is still more vital to us: that is, the governing principles, the governing factors. We have seen that to possess the good land, to enter into the all-inclusiveness of Christ, cannot be accomplished by an individual person but only by a collective people. This is quite clear. But we must realize that especially with a collective people, the need exists for some governing principles. There must be *order*. In a corporate body, things must be put into order. If there are no governing principles, disorder and confusion will reign, and disorder and confusion are akin to the enemy. If we are out of order, we are spoiled and we are linked with Satan. Hence, it is impossible for us to enter into the good land. In order to maintain order among the Lord's children, there must be some governing principles, some governing factors.

In these two books, Exodus and Leviticus, we not only see the various items of the enjoyment of Christ, but also the governing principles which God has ordained among His children. There are at least three important and vital governing factors or principles.

THE PRESENCE OF THE LORD

The first governing principle is the presence of the Lord in the pillar of cloud and the pillar of fire. I do not only say the pillar of cloud and pillar of fire, but *the presence of the Lord* in the pillar of cloud and in the pillar of fire. In these pillars, the presence of the Lord is the first governing principle. This factor relates to the gathering and to the activity or movement of the Lord's people. When, how, and where the Lord's people should move and act depends on the presence of the Lord revealed to them in the pillar of cloud and in the pillar of fire. In other words, if we would go on to possess the land, we must do so by the presence of the Lord. If the presence of the Lord goes with us, we can enter and enjoy the land. You remember how the Lord promised Moses, "My presence shall go with you, and I will give you rest" (Exo. 33:14). This means that He would bring the people into the possession of the land by His presence. So Moses said to the Lord, "If Your presence does not go with us, do not bring us up from here" (v. 15). Moses demanded that the Lord's presence must go with them; otherwise, he would not go.

"My presence shall go with you." This is quite a peculiar word. *The presence* shall go. It does not mean that He will go. *He will go* is one thing, and *His presence shall go* is another. Do you realize the difference?

Let me illustrate with a story. One time four or five of us who were serving the Lord together were going to a certain place. We all traveled together. One brother at that time, however, was not happy with us, yet he had no choice but to go. We all traveled on the same train: all but this one brother sat in car number one, and he sat by himself in car number two. He went with us, but his presence did not go with us. He left with us, he traveled with us, and he arrived with us, but his presence was not with us. When the brothers came to welcome us, he was there, and through all of our visit in that place, he was there. He was with us, but his presence was not. It was indeed strange.

Brothers and sisters, many times the Lord will go with you, but His presence will not. Many times the Lord will truly help you, but be assured, He is not happy with you. You will receive His help, but you will lose His presence. He will bring you to your destination and He will bless you, but throughout the whole trip you will not sense His presence. *He* will go with you, but *His presence* will not.

Oh, this is not a theory, but our real experience! Many times in past years while I was serving the Lord, I have realized His help. The Lord is bound to help me; He must help me for His own sake. But I can tell you that many times I did not have the presence of the Lord, simply because He was not happy with me. He had to go with me, but He was not happy. I was sitting in car number one, but He was sitting in car number two. He went along, but He withheld His presence that I might know His displeasure.

Some years ago a young sister spoke with me about her marriage. She said, "Brother, I feel it is the Lord's will that I become engaged to a certain gentleman. The Lord has really helped me in this matter, so at a certain date we will announce our engagement." I knew something of the situation, so I said to the sister, "No doubt the Lord has helped you—I do believe your word. But is the Lord happy with you in this matter? Is the Lord's presence with you as you contemplate this engagement?" "Oh, brother," she replied, "to tell you the truth, I know the Lord is not happy with me. I know it! On one hand, He has helped me, but on the other hand, I know He is not happy with me." "How do you know?" I asked. Her answer is most significant: "Whenever I think about it, I sense that I have lost His presence." This is an excellent illustration. The Lord helped her, but He withheld His presence.

Brothers and sisters, you must be clear. Never think that as long as the Lord helps you, it is sufficient. No, no! Far from it. We must have the Lord's presence. We must learn to pray: "Lord, if You will not give me Your presence, I will stay here with You. If Your presence does not go with me, I will not go. I will not be governed by Your help, but by Your presence." We must go even further to pray, "O Lord, I do not want Your help, but I do want Your presence. Lord, I must have Your presence. I can do without Your help, but I cannot do without Your presence." Can you say this to the Lord?

Many brothers and sisters come to me, saying, "Oh, brother, the Lord has really helped me!" I always wish to ask them, "Have you sensed the presence of the Lord? You have gotten His help, but have you sensed His presence?" Many get the help of the Lord, but few have the presence of the Lord. His help is not the governing factor, but His presence.

Some Christian workers have said to me, "Brother, do you not realize that the Lord has helped us? Do you not believe that the Lord has blessed us?" "Undoubtedly," I have answered, "the Lord has helped you and blessed you, but let us be silent for a little while before the Lord." After a while, I have asked, "Brother, do you feel in your deepest sense that you have the presence of the Lord with you? I know that you have done something for the Lord; I know that the Lord has helped you and blessed you. But I wish to know, in the innermost part of your being, do you feel that the Lord is so present with you? Do you always sense His face smiling upon you, and has the very smile of the Lord entered into you? Do you have this?" These are tender and heart-searching words. As a servant of the Lord, most people cannot tell a lie; they must tell the truth. Eventually, such brothers have said, "I must tell you, for some time I have lost my fellowship with the Lord." Then I asked, "Brother, what is this? Are you governed by the help of the Lord or by His presence? Are you governed by His blessing or by His smile?"

Brothers and sisters, though it be with tears in our eyes, we must say day by day, "Lord, nothing but Your smiling presence will satisfy me. I do not want anything but the smile of Your glorious face. As long as I have this, I care not whether the heaven comes down or the earth falls apart. The whole world may rise against me, but as long as I have Your smile upon me, I can praise You, and everything is well." The Lord said, "My *presence* shall go with you." What a treasure! The presence, the smile, of the Lord is the governing principle. We must be fearful of receiving anything from the Lord yet losing His presence. This is indeed a fearful thing. The Lord Himself may very well give you something, and yet that very thing will rob you of His presence. He will help you, He will bless you, and yet that very help and blessing can keep you away from His presence. We must learn to be kept, to be ruled, to be governed, to be guided simply by the presence of the Lord. We must tell the Lord that we do not want anything but His direct presence. We do not want His presence second-hand. Many times, be assured, you have the secondhand presence of the Lord; it is not firsthand, it is not direct. Try to be governed by the direct, firsthand presence of the Lord.

This is not only a requirement and a qualification but also a power for you to go on to possess the land. The firsthand presence of the Lord will strengthen you with might to obtain the fullness, the all-inclusiveness of Christ. Oh, what a strength, what a power is in the direct presence of the Lord! This is certainly not a matter of doctrine, but of our innermost experience.

"My presence shall go with you." The Lord is so wonderful, so glorious, so mysterious! But in what way does He show us His presence? How is His presence realized by us? In the ancient time, His presence was always in the cloud by day and the fire by night, in the pillar of cloud and the pillar of fire. During the day while the sun was shining, the cloud was there; in the darkness of the night, there was the fire. The Lord's presence revealed to His children in the day was the cloud and in the night was the fire.

What do these two things, the cloud and the fire, mean? Several passages in the Scriptures show that the cloud is the symbol of the Spirit. The Holy Spirit in our experience is sometimes just like a cloud. The presence of the Lord is in the Spirit. Many times we know that the presence of the Lord is with us. How do we know it? Because we realize it in the Spirit. I believe that most of us have had some experience of this. We have experienced the presence of the Lord in the Spirit. It is indeed mysterious. If you ask how you may experience the presence of the Lord in the Spirit, I can only answer that I experience it, I realize it. The Lord is in the Spirit, and His presence is realized by me in the Spirit. The reality is in the Spirit. Sometimes—it may be due to our weakness, or it may be that the Lord feels we need encouragement or confirmation—He gives us some apprehension and even some feeling that the Spirit is really like a cloud.

In 1935 I was delivering a message concerning the out-pouring of the Holy Spirit. During the middle of the message, I suddenly had the sensation of a cloud enveloping me. It seemed that I was in a cloud. Immediately the meeting took a definite turn, and the words which issued from my mouth were just as living water pouring out. The whole congregation was astonished. When you have such an experience, you need not speak anything by your mind. The words flow out from the Spirit.

That is the presence of the Lord in the pillar of the cloud. You can sense it in such a way. It comes as a kind of guidance and encouragement. You are burdened with something for the Lord, and the Lord gives you such an encouragement to let you sense His presence in the Spirit. This, however, is a spe-cial experience bestowed by the Lord. Day by day we can experience the Lord's presence in the Spirit in a normal and ordinary way.

What then is the meaning of the pillar of fire? We need the fire in the night, when it is dark. But the meaning is the same as that of the cloud. The cloud is the fire, and the fire is the cloud. When the sun shines, the Lord's presence takes the appearance of a cloud; when darkness comes, it takes the appearance of fire. It is the same entity with different appear-ances. Then what does the fire represent? It represents the Word. The cloud is the Spirit, and the fire is the Word. When the sun is shining, you are very clear in the Spirit; you can easily follow the cloud. But many times it is just like night, and you are in darkness. You cannot trust your spirit; your spirit is very much perplexed. In such a situation you must trust the Word. The Word is like the fire, burning, shining, and enlightening. Psalm 119:105 says, "Your word is a lamp to my feet / And a light to my path." When the sky is so clear and everything is so bright, the cloud is adequate. But when dark-ness veils the sky, you cannot discern which is the cloud and which is not the cloud; you must follow the fire. Sometimes your sky, your day, is exceedingly clear, and the sunlight is bright and strong. You can see unmistakably the way the Spirit is going and follow accordingly. But more often, probably, you are in darkness, you are in the night. Yesterday you were so clear, but today you are so darkened; you are puzzled and perplexed. But do not worry—you have the Word. Follow the Word. The Word is the fire, the burning fire, the bright light. You can follow this light when you are in darkness, for the Lord's presence is in the fire.

Many times brothers have said to me, "Brother, I am in darkness now." "Praise the Lord!" I reply. "This is just the right time for you to take the Word. If you were not in darkness, there would be no opportunity for you to experience the Lord in the Word. Just take His Word." How good it is to experience Christ in His Word when we are in darkness.

The Lord's presence is always in these two things, either in the Spirit or in the Word. When you are clear, you can realize that He is in the Spirit. When you are in darkness, you can see Him in the Word. He is always in these two: in the Spirit and in the Word. Are you clear today? Praise the Lord! You will sense the Lord in the Spirit. Are you in darkness? You can praise Him too, for you can see Him in His Word. Sometimes we are in the day with the sunshine, and sometimes we are in the night with the darkness. But we need not be concerned. In the day, when it is clear, we have the Spirit as the cloud; in the night, when it is dark, we have the Word as the fire. We can follow the Lord by His presence in the Spirit and in the Word.

THE PRIESTHOOD WITH THE URIM
AND THE THUMMIM

The second governing principle is the priesthood under the anointing with the Urim and the Thummim. What is the priesthood? This is a wonderful and glorious matter. The priesthood includes fellowship with the Lord and life and service in His presence. The priesthood is a group of people who are in constant fellowship with the Lord. They continually commune with the Lord and serve in His presence. They live, walk, and do everything in this way. When we have fellowship with the Lord, when we commune with the Lord day by day and moment by moment, and when in this living fellowship we live, we serve, and we act, we are a priesthood.

If we lose the priesthood, we lose one of the governing

principles. This governing principle is not for guidance, but for judgment. The Lord's presence in the pillars of cloud and fire is for guidance, while the priesthood in the anointing with the Urim and Thummim is for judgment.

Let us illustrate. Suppose two brothers are quarreling and fighting with one another. What shall we do? We are the Lord's children, we are the Lord's people, but something of such a nature exists among us. How can we solve the problem? How can we arrive at the proper judgment? Shall we call a meeting and decide the matter by vote? Of course not. All such problems can only be solved by the priesthood. They require a group of the Lord's children who are always in fellowship with the Lord, who serve the Lord in His presence and who are continually before Him, no matter where they are or what they are doing. Such a group is under the anointing of the Holy Spirit and has the Urim and the Thummim. Thus, they can obtain the judgment, the decision of the Lord. They will be able to judge and decide any matter that may arise by the Urim and Thummim with the priesthood.

The priesthood includes three things: communion or fellowship with the Lord, the anointing of the Holy Spirit, and the Urim and Thummim. We can only speak briefly here concerning the last item, the Urim and the Thummim. Urim in Hebrew means "light," while Thummim means "perfection, or completion." About thirty years ago I read an article by a Hebrew writer, saying that the Thummim is a precious stone with four letters of the Hebrew alphabet carved upon it. Upon the breastplate of the high priests were the names of the twelve tribes of Israel carved upon twelve stones. The names of these twelve tribes contain only eighteen of the twenty-two letters in the Hebrew alphabet. Therefore, upon the breastplate of the high priest there was a shortage of four letters. However, these four letters were carved upon the Thummim, and when this stone was put into the breastplate, there was perfection, there was completion. There were then the full twenty-two letters. All the letters of the Hebrew alphabet were there. Then we are told that the Urim is a stone put into the breastplate to give light. Hence, we have the meaning of the Urim and Thummim: light and perfection.

How then were the Urim and the Thummim used? When some problem or question arose among the children of Israel, the high priest brought the matter to the Lord to get the answer by the help of the breastplate. The Hebrew writer in this article says that when the high priests went before the Lord, certain stones on the breastplate with their respective letters would shine and at other times other stones with their letters would shine. The high priest took down all the letters from the various stones as they shone, and in so doing formed words and then sentences. Eventually he received a complete message or judgment from the Lord. It was in this way, the article says, that Achan was apprehended from among all the children of Israel for his sin (Josh. 7).

Thus, what is the governing principle for the Lord's people to solve their problems? It is that among them there should be the priesthood that brings all the Lord's children upon the breast before the Lord. The priesthood must bring them in love into the Lord's presence and read them there as letters. Thus, with the light of the Scriptures, the priesthood will learn the mind of the Lord and receive some word from Him regarding the situation of His children.

Now regarding the brothers who are quarreling with each other, we have the answer. We can tell them, "Brothers, be quiet for some time. We will go to the Lord." We will then bring this problem to the Lord and read these brothers in His presence with the light of the Scriptures. This is the exercise of the priesthood with the breastplate of the Urim and the Thummim. By this we can get the letters, the words, and the message of the Lord regarding what decision must be made in this matter.

Do you know how the apostles wrote their Epistles? It was exactly in this way. The first Epistle of Paul to the Corinthians is a good example. Paul was confronted with many problems in that church: problems of sectarianism, discipline, marriage, the doctrine of resurrection, etc. There were problems of almost every kind and description. What did he do? He brought all the problems and all the brothers and sisters in that church upon his heart to the Lord, and in the presence of the Lord he read them with the light of the Scriptures. Is this not true? As he read them there by the light of the Word, he realized the nature of the situation and the answer. He received a judgment, a decision from the Lord, and so he wrote the first Epistle to the Corinthians. Consider all the Epistles. All the books written by the apostles were done in such a way. It was not that they sat in their room reading, reasoning, and then writing. No. There was always some situation among the Lord's children which demanded an answer, a word from the Lord. Then the apostles as priests fulfilling their priestly ministry brought all these problems with all the Lord's children into God's presence. They studied the problem in His presence, reading the believers one by one in the light of the Lord's words. Thus, they received light; they got words, sentences, and thoughts from the Lord. Then they wrote the letters, telling the saints the Lord's mind.

This is one of the governing principles. The first ruling principle is the presence of the Lord in the pillar of cloud and pillar of fire, and the second is the priesthood under the anointing with these two peculiar things, the Urim and the Thummim.

Brothers and sisters, if you come to me telling of some problem you have with others, what should I do? I should exercise my spirit to bring you and the others to the Lord. With love I should put you and those other brothers or sisters on my heart, that is, upon my breast. I should bring all of you to the Lord and say, "Lord, here are some dear saints. Illuminate them. Give me Your light." I should read you. I should read your minds and your emotions. I should read your thoughts, your motives, and your actions. I should read your problem and many things related to you in the light of the Word. After reading letter by letter, I will gradually get a word and then another word. Eventually I will receive a sentence and then a message. I will know something from the Lord. I will know what is the Lord's mind toward you and His thought about you.

You who are leading brothers meet many kinds of problems in the church which give you opportunity to practice this priestly ministry. Sometimes a brother will come to you to share a problem he has with his father, who is also a brother in the Lord. He will ask you what he should do. The next day a sister may come to you telling of some trouble she has with her sister-in-law, who is also a sister in the church. What will you do? Will you tell them to go to court and see the judge? Of course, you cannot do that. The only way is just as we have shown. You must have a heart; you must have a breast; you must have love. Put them on your heart and bring them thus to the Lord. Exercise your spirit and read them before the Lord. Read the father first, and then read the son. Read their habits, their nationalities, their characters, their thoughts, their education—not by your way of thinking, but by the light of the Word. Read all these things. After reading, you will receive the sentences and the language, point by point. You will get a word from the Lord which will reveal to you His mind. Then you will be able to speak to the son and his father. Do the same with the sister and her sister-in-law. You will be able to say to them, "This is the Lord's mind. Pray about it." You have obtained the judgment and the decision from the Lord. This is the court for the Lord's people. We do need such a court. We need a local representation of the heavenly supreme court. The court is the priesthood under the anointing of the Holy Spirit with the Urim and the Thummim.

It is not a small thing to have a group of the Lord's children who are coordinated together to serve the Lord collectively. It is not so simple. Consider your own family. Do you not have some kind of family court to settle all your problems? What is our family court in the church? It is simply the priesthood, the fellowship with the Lord under the anointing of the Holy Spirit in reading all the brothers and sisters by the light of the Word. In this way we receive the judgment and make the decisions for all our affairs. All our problems and questions are solved in this way. It is not by arguing; it is not by consulting, reasoning, and arranging as a politician or an earthly judge. It is only by fellowship and anointing, reading in love the circumstances, natures, and daily lives of the believers with the light of the Lord's Word.

THE REGULATIONS OF A HOLY LIFE

The third governing factor is the regulations of a holy life.

What are these regulations? In the book of Leviticus, we have the offerings, the priesthood, and many kinds of regulations. Leviticus can be divided into these three parts: the first, dealing with the offerings, is from chapters 1 through 7; the second, dealing with the priesthood, is from chapters 8 to 10; the third, from chapter 11 through the end of the book, deals with many regulations. There are all kinds of regulations regarding a holy life, a holy living. We cannot go into detail now regarding them all. If we could, we would see how interesting, how sweet, and how pregnant with meaning they are. There are many regulations about what is clean and what is unclean, about what is separated and what is not separated from common and worldly things, about how to act and how not to act. All these are regulations for a holy life.

These regulations can be summed up for the sake of simplicity into three minor principles. The first is that we are the people who belong to the Lord. This is a minor principle which must regulate us. Remember that you belong to the Lord; you are the Lord's people. If you remember this, you will be kept from many things. Do you think that while remembering you are the Lord's people, you could attend a theater? The very thought will make you shrink from it. Do you think that you can quarrel with someone and at the same time remember that you belong to the Lord? Try it. You will see what will become of your quarrel.

One time in the Far East I engaged a rickshaw man for a ride. He told me at first that he would charge five dollars, to which I agreed. When I arrived at my destination, however, I saw that I only had a ten dollar bill, so I handed it to him and waited for the change. After looking around in his pockets, he eventually said he was sorry, for he only had four dollars with which to refund me. This is their trick. I began to quarrel with him, but suddenly I remembered that I was a child of God. Just this remembrance caused me to drop it. I said, "All right, all right, forget it; one dollar does not matter." How could I who am a child of the Lord argue with a rickshaw boy? That would put the name of the Lord to shame.

Whenever you are about to do something, you must remember that you are one of the Lord's children. Do not say that this is too legal. You and I must be legal in such a way. Sometimes the sisters, especially in the Far East, wear dresses which are really not becoming to a child of the Lord. If they would only remember that they belong to the Lord, the very thought would cause them to shrink from such attire. They simply forget that they are children of the Lord and proceed to dress like daughters of the devil. To remember that we are the Lord's people is the first minor principle of the regulations.

The second is that we have been separated from this world. The Lord said, "I have set you apart from the peoples" (Lev. 20:26). We have been separated from the peoples of the world by the Lord. What they can do, we cannot. What they can say, we cannot. What they can possess, we cannot. Many times I have gone to the department store and have been unable to buy anything. All I could do was shake my head and say, "No, no, there is nothing for me. I am separated."

From Seattle to San Francisco and then to Los Angeles I have been trying to get a pair of shoes. There are so many peculiar and modern styles, it is rather difficult to find a suitable pair as a child of God. If I were to buy some of them, I fear that I would not be able to stand and minister to the Lord's children. Oh, the things, the worldly things these department stores are selling! If all the worldly people would be converted and remember that they are children of the Lord and separated from this world, all the department stores would be forced to close. There would be no business for them. It is regrettable that the majority of people are not converted, but the greatest pity is that those who are converted by the Lord are still not separated from this world. At least we who are converted by the Lord must remember that we are those whom the Lord has separated from this world. This is also one of the principles which must govern us. Do not say that this is too legal. We must be so legal.

The third minor principle is that the Lord is holy, so we too must be holy. The Lord is separated and different from all other things, so we too must be sanctified from all things. We must be holy in all things just as He is holy.

These three minor principles compose one of the major

governing principles, and these are the regulations of a holy life. What are they? First, remember that you are the Lord's children; second, remember that you have been separated from this world; third, remember that your God is a holy God and you must be just as holy as He. These three regulations should govern everything in your life.

In conclusion, the Lord's presence is the guidance for us as a group. Whether we should go or stay, we may know by the presence of the Lord. We must be guided by nothing but His presence. This is the first governing principle. Then, if there is some problem among us, we need not seek any solution in an outward way. We have the court of the priesthood. By the fellowship among us with the Lord under the anointing of the Holy Spirit and through the studying with love of all the brothers and sisters in the light of the Word, we may obtain the needed judgment, the proper decision. This is the second govern ing principle. As to our daily life and daily activities, we must be always ruled by the remembrance that we are the Lord's children, that we are separated from this world, and that we must be holy as the Lord is holy. This is the third governing principle. If we are ruled by these principles, we will be prepared and qualified to go on to possess that good land; we will be enabled to enter into the all-inclusiveness of Christ.

CHAPTER TWELVE

HOW TO POSSESS THE LAND

(4)

BY THE FORMATION OF THE ARMY

Scripture Reading: Num. 1:1-4, 17, 18, 52, 53; 2:1, 2; 4:3; 8:23-26; 26:1, 2, 52-56, 63-65

We have seen many things regarding the entering of the good land. They are all related to the enjoyment of Christ, starting with the enjoyment of Him as the passover lamb to the enjoyment of Him as the Ark enlarged with the tabernacle, including the offerings and the priesthood. At this point in our experience, we are rather matured; thus, we are in the position to assume some responsibility. It is at this stage that we are able to function in the priesthood, which means that to a certain degree we can serve God.

FROM EXODUS TO NUMBERS

Everything in the book of Exodus is presented in a progressive way. From the starting point of enjoying Christ as the passover lamb, the children of Israel went on until one day the tabernacle was reared up among them. It was then that they enjoyed Christ as the testimony of God, and at that stage they could take responsibility for God as priests. This is the book of Exodus.

Following Exodus, we come to Leviticus, where Christ is seen as so many offerings to be enjoyed. God's people may thus enjoy Christ in a much fuller way than before. They can then bear the full responsibility of the priesthood and realize all the divine regulations concerning the holy life. We have seen that in Leviticus there are three portions: the first deals with the offerings, the second with the priesthood, and the last with the divine principles of the holy life.

After Leviticus, we come to Numbers. Most expositions and commentaries on this part of the Bible declare that Numbers is a book wholly occupied with the numbering and the wandering of the children of Israel. Apparently this is true, but in essence it is not. Although this element exists, yet principally and spiritually it is a book of glorious records. It is a book which records the formation of the divine army. Only at this point, after the experiences of Exodus and Leviticus, is it possible for the people of God to be formed into an army to fight the battle for Him. It is indeed glorious that a group of the Lord's children could be formed into an army for the Lord on this earth. And it is further glorious that these very people are those who will take possession of the land. Those who are able to fight the battle for God are those who will divide and take possession of the land.

In the book of Numbers, the people of Israel were numbered twice. They were numbered the first time to be formed as an army to fight the battle. They were numbered the second time, not only as an army for the warfare, but also as a people to divide and inherit the good land. Those who share the land are those who fight the battle. In this book, therefore, we may realize not only the numberings or the wanderings but the glorious fact of being formed as an army and designated to inherit the good land.

FROM THE LAMB TO AN ARMY—A CHECK LIST

What then is the way to possess the good land? It is not so simple. Let us enumerate and review the steps. First of all, we must enjoy Christ as the redeeming lamb. We must receive Christ as our Savior. We must pass the judgment of God. This is the first step. If we have done this, we can put a check here; the first item has been passed. What is the second step? We must leave Egypt and enjoy Christ as our daily manna, as our daily life supply. Of course, we cannot take food without drinking water, so at the same time we must enjoy Christ as the rock with the living water flowing forth. We enjoy the manna and we enjoy the rock with the living water.

Do you have such an experience day by day? Many of you can boldly say that you do. Every day you enjoy Christ as your food and as your drink. Otherwise, you could not live, you could not go on, you could not maintain your life as a Christian. Day by day we must enjoy Christ as our daily food and our living water; we must have something to eat and something to drink. Whenever we meet in the morning, instead of greeting one another with "Good morning!" let us ask, "Have you eaten?" I do prefer such a greeting. Have you eaten this morning, brother? Have you drunk something this morning, sister? Some of you can answer that you have had three good meals today. Praise the Lord! We must tell people that day by day we are feeding on Christ. We are eating Christ and we are drinking Christ. If we have this experience, we can check this also.

Now let us come to the third. Do you have a tabernacle where you live? And do you enjoy Christ as the center, as the testimony of God among you? Do you really experience Christ as the manifestation and the explanation of God in a solid way, as well as the expansion of Christ, the tabernacle, as His real expression among you? Do you have this experience in the locality where you live? Do you have a tabernacle with such a Christ, not only as the lamb or as the daily manna, but as the testimony of God? Or is there some problem at this point? In other words, is there a group of people in your city who experience Christ as the manifestation of God with the increase of Himself, the church, as His real expression? What is your answer? Perhaps some are beginning to have this experience. If so, praise the Lord! Perhaps many must confess that they have nothing in this way.

The first item, of course, is easily passed. Concerning the second, there may be some doubt. With the third, however, there is a considerable problem. The experience of the Ark with the tabernacle is rare indeed. What then can we do? Brothers and sisters, we must pray. You who live together in a certain city must come together to pray for this matter. Pray that the Lord will reveal to you and cause you to experience Christ, the very testimony of God, as your center as well as the church, the enlargement of Himself, as His expression.

This is not a teaching to be stored in your mind. You must realize your actual situation before the Lord and deal with Him about this matter. You must pray that a spiritual tabernacle be reared up where you are, that there will be a new beginning. This is not a small thing; it is an entirely new start. At a certain point, something new must be started among you. Formerly, all you have enjoyed has been Christ as the lamb, as the manna, and at the most as the rock with the living water. Now you must enjoy Christ in a new way, in a new stage, so that there will be a new start of the Spirit among you. You must come to "the first day of the first month...in the second year" that the tabernacle, the church, might be reared up (Exo. 40:2, 17). This is a new beginning in the second stage. You have already begun in the first year in the first stage. Now you must start the second year in the second stage. You must go on to have Christ as your center and the tabernacle as His expression raised up in your locality.

Let us come now to the fourth item. Suppose we have the tabernacle here. Then we must go on to experience Christ in a much richer way. We must experience Him as all the offerings—as the trespass offering, as the sin offering, as the peace offering, as the meal offering, and as the burnt offering.

The fifth item is the experience of Christ as the high priest so that we can assume the priesthood. What about this? Can you say that you have a real priesthood in your locality? Perhaps you have been able to check all the items so far. But can you check this one? This is a deeper experience.

The thought or line of the Holy Spirit in the record of the Scriptures is always progressive, is always improving. From the first to the second, to the third, to the fourth, and now to the fifth, there is a steady improving, solidifying, and deepening. But if most of you speak honestly before the Lord, you must confess that it is rather difficult to pass this fifth item. Not many groups of the Lord's children ever realize the priesthood. Is there a priesthood in your city? Take time to consider all these items one by one. Then you will know where you are.

At the present time one can hardly find a group of the

Lord's people who have come to this stage, who have enjoyed Christ as the high priest to such an extent that they have taken up the priesthood. In our prayers we say, "O Lord, You are our high priest!" But this is just words; we do not have the experience. We have not experienced very much regarding Christ as the high priest, so we are not able to assume the priesthood. We must know what the priesthood means to us and to God.

Now we come to the sixth item. We must be formed into an army. This is a further development. We as a group of the Lord's children must be formed into an army to fight the battle for Him on this earth. Oh, this is tremendous! If this strikes fear in you, you may turn back. This is indeed a matter of universal significance.

Brothers and sisters, you must take all these matters most seriously. You must pray together: "Lord, do we know something of experiencing You as the Ark, the testimony of God, with its expansion as Your expression?" Check with the Lord and learn by His grace to apply Christ in this very aspect. Then ask the Lord, "Do we have some experience of You as the high priest so that we are able to assume the priesthood among Your people?" By the grace of the Lord, learn it and experience it; apply Christ as the priesthood life.

QUALIFICATIONS FOR THE ARMY

Then, following the priesthood, we need the formation of the army. By the assuming of the priesthood, we can be formed into a spiritual army to fight for the Lord's interest on this earth. Some qualifications, however, are required whereby we may be formed into such an army. First, to be formed into an army, everyone must give his pedigree, his genealogy—not physical, of course, but spiritual. No physical genealogy will suffice for this. We must have a spiritual genealogy. The children of Israel had to state their pedigree. They had to declare their father and to what family and tribe they belonged. If they could not make such a declaration, if they could not give their pedigree, they must stand back; they could not be formed into the army. You must have spiritual life. Are you born again? Then give us your pedigree. At least you must tell the name of your father. This means that you must check your rebirth. Do you have the assurance that you have spiritual life? Are you a real Israelite? We must be assured that we are born again.

Recently I had a talk with a young brother. I asked him how old he was, and he answered that he was thirteen years of age. Then I asked him when he was saved, and he replied that he was saved when he was nine. "How do you know you were saved?" I asked. "Because I met the Holy Spirit; when I was nine years of age I met the Holy Spirit." He could give me something as a spiritual pedigree to prove that he had been born again. He had the life of a real Israelite. He had the start. This is the first condition for being formed into the army.

Now the second. You have the birth, you have the life, but you must have a certain amount of growth; you must be twenty years of age (Num. 1:3). A soldier must be someone with a matured life. Babies cannot be sent to war. We must be spiritually matured to twenty years of age. This is the growth and maturity of the spiritual life. Can you say that there are some among you who are truly matured, who can stand up to fight the battle for the kingdom of God? In many places there are many Christians, but it seems that they are just like children playing with spiritual things. They are so young. They can give you their spiritual pedigree, but they have not grown. To make matters worse, though they are infants, yet in their estimation they are the greatest.

One day the granddaughter of a brother said to me, "Don't call me 'baby.' I am big!" She was just three years of age, and she loved to think how big she was. Can you send a child like that to war? Ridiculous! We must grow in the spiritual life. We must grow up to a certain standard that we may be formed into an army to fight the battle for the kingdom and the testimony of God.

Allow me to repeat that this is not a teaching. You must pray about this matter. Pray and remember that you must grow to a certain standard. The standard can never be lowered. We must grow up to it. I say *grow up,* not *grow old.* If you become old, you will be discharged; you will be retired from spiritual service. You must only advance; you must never deteriorate. You must stand in the army from the age of twenty to the age of sixty. You must be full of experience, but void of deterioration. Some, indeed, have not yet grown up, but they are already old. They are old young ones. We must grow to a certain stage of life to be formed into the army. This is the second qualification.

The third is that all the people of Israel must be under their own standard according to their houses. This means they have no choice. If you are from San Francisco, you must remain under the standard of San Francisco. If you are from Los Angeles, you must remain under the standard of Los Angeles. You have no option. Perhaps you were born in Los Angeles, but you feel unhappy with the brothers and sisters in that city. You would like to move. You think you would be more happy with the brothers and sisters in San Francisco. But the Lord says, "Go back; return to your father's house; return to the standard of that house." This means your personal tastes, your personal desires, your personal choices must be dealt with. There are no personal choices among the people of God. I cannot say that I am of the tribe of Judah, but I do not like this tribe; I prefer Benjamin. I must remain under the standard of Judah. My own desire must be limited.

Look at the situation today among the Lord's children. How much confusion there is! Those from the tribe of "Judah" have come under the standard of "Benjamin," and those of the tribe of "Benjamin" have moved to "Manasseh." Everything is in a state of chaos. It is impossible for an army to be formed in such a situation. We must have the life, we must have the growth, and we must be limited by the standard of our father's house. This is a strict lesson for us to learn.

Fourth, we must be in order. Consider the picture of the children of Israel. In the center was the Ark with its enlargement, the tabernacle. Around the tabernacle were encamped the Levites, family by family. Then, surrounding them, all the other twelve tribes were positioned and encamped. They kept the order. There was a place for every tribe. Certain tribes were ordained to camp on the east, certain tribes on the south, others on the west, and some on the north. The order of

the Lord involves the matter of submission. If we would keep
the order, we must learn the lesson of submission. We must
submit ourselves to somebody; otherwise, there is no possibil-
ity for the army to be formed. When we grow in life to be
formed as the army of God to fight the battle for His kingdom, we will spontaneously be submissive. Every one of us
will be submissive to others. There will be a divine order among
us; hence, an army will be formed.

This is the way for us to possess the good land, the
all-inclusive Christ. You can take no other way. The only way
is to enjoy Christ as the lamb, as the manna, as the rock with
the living water, as the Ark with the tabernacle, as the offerings, as the priest in order to assume the priesthood, and
lastly to grow up to be formed into an army.

The fifth qualification is that we must always be fresh
and young. Whenever we begin to get old, we must be
renewed. By the time of the second numbering, all those from
the first numbering had grown old. Thus, they must be numbered again. The old ones passed away and the new ones
came in. Those who can be formed into an army among the
children of God and share the good land are those who are
continually young and fresh.

Indeed, not all the people of Israel were formed into the
army. There were those who did not qualify because they
were women. A woman in the Scripture means a "weaker,
female vessel" (1 Pet. 3:7). They typify the weak ones among
the Lord's children. And there were those who were below the
age of twenty, the immature. Not all, by any means, are qualified for the army. Do not expect that all the brothers and
sisters among you will be included in the army. There may be
just two or three, four or five, nine or ten. There may be just a
small group as a nucleus. But, praise the Lord, as long as
there are a few who truly have the growth of life, you may
take the ground to be formed as an army. You may tell the
Lord that you are there in that city to be an army to fight the
battle for Him.

We must be clear, however, that before we can be an army,
we must first assume the priesthood. Look at the picture. In
the center is the Ark with the tabernacle. Then, around the

tabernacle is the priesthood. Next, surrounding the priesthood is the army. We must move from the center to the circumference. If we do not know how to keep the fellowship with the Lord, we will be unable to fight. Spiritual fighting always depends upon spiritual fellowship. By maintaining the priesthood, we will be able to fight the battle. If we lose our fellowship with the Lord, we can do nothing with the enemy; we will be defeated.

In Numbers 4:3, 30, 35, 39, and 43, the word *service,* related to the service of the priesthood, is the same word in Hebrew as *military service* in Numbers 26:2, related to the warfare of the army. The priests must perform their service in the tabernacle, but their service is referred to as a warfare. While they are serving, they are fighting the battle. In other words, the priestly service is the warfare. If we are really in the priesthood today, we will simultaneously be the army. To be out of the priesthood is to be out of the army. To maintain the priesthood is to maintain the warfare. The army is always kept by the priesthood.

Do we have the spiritual pedigree? Do we have the adequate growth of spiritual life? Do we take the limitation to our personal tastes, our personal desires, and our personal choices among the Lord's children? If we can answer "Yes," then we must keep the order with submission and we must always be fresh. Then we will be enabled to assume the priesthood and be formed into an army.

Oh, brothers and sisters, how short we come! By checking item by item, it seems that when we come to item five concerning the priesthood we cannot get through. If we cannot get through with item five, we certainly cannot get through with item six. We must pray. We must seek to apply Christ as the high priest and learn to assume the priesthood. Then we can make some advance in being formed as the army of the Lord to fight the battle for the kingdom of God.

We must notice one further matter. The requirement for service in the army is twenty years of age, while the requirement of the priesthood is thirty years of age. The duration of service in the army is from twenty to sixty years of age, while in the priesthood it is from thirty to fifty years of age. In both the army and the priesthood there must be full growth without any kind of deterioration. Both the priesthood and the army depend upon the growth in life. We must take this seriously. We must grow; otherwise, there will be no priesthood and no army among us. How the Lord's children need to grow! May the Lord open our eyes and show us how much we need the growth of life. Only by growing to a certain standard can we assume the responsibility of the priesthood and be formed into an army. Only then can we be spiritually organized into a people with the Ark as the center, the tabernacle as its enlargement, and everyone kept in order with submission. It is a beautiful picture. Then we will be ready to cross the river Jordan and take possession of the land.

We have been speaking very much about the all-inclusive land, the all-inclusive Christ. This is the way to possess it; this is the way to enter in. All the records of these three books—Exodus, Leviticus, and Numbers—deal with the steps to possess the good land. We may say that there are six steps. The first two are comparatively easy to pass. It is the last four that pose a great problem—the tabernacle with the Ark as the center, the offerings, the priesthood, and the formation of the army. Let us pray and be deeply exercised before the Lord that we might advance in the spiritual life, that we might go on from the experience of Christ as the lamb all the way to the priesthood and the army.

Chapter Thirteen

HOW TO POSSESS THE LAND

(5)

THE OPPOSING FACTORS

Scripture Reading: Lev. 10:1-3; Num. 12:1, 2, 9, 10, 15; 13:2—
14:10; 16:1-3, 12-14; 21:5, 6; 25:1-5; 26:63-65; 1 Cor. 10:1-6; Heb.
4:11

In this chapter we will see how to possess the land from
the negative aspect instead of from the positive. This will be
more helpful to us.

INDEPENDENCE AND INDIVIDUALISM

We have seen that the way for the Lord's people to possess
the good land is in a group, not as single persons. This means
that not one person as an individual can enter this land. It is
not his business. It is the business of a collective body. We
have seen this quite clearly. I must also remind you once more
that in order for the people of the Lord to enter the good land,
they must have the tabernacle. The first thing that the children of Israel set up among them was the tabernacle. This
very fact indicates graphically that the entrance into the land
is a collective matter, not an individual one. In order to possess the good land, we must be built up; we must all be united
into one body as the tabernacle.

We have seen quite clearly that the enjoyment of Christ is
a progression, a continual development. There is a start, and
there is a process; there is a way to improve and advance. We
started at the very beginning by enjoying Christ as the lamb.
Then by going on we attain to the point where Christ to us

is the Ark of the Testimony with the increase of the tabernacle. This increase, this enlargement of the Ark, is a group of people mingled with Christ and built up together in the divine nature. They are built into one body as the very expression of Christ, who is the manifestation and testimony of God. We must be very clear that at this stage these people who have been continually enjoying Christ have become one. They are no longer simply individuals; by the enjoyment of Christ they have become one body. At the very beginning it seems that we enjoy Christ separately and individually. You enjoy Christ as the lamb, and I enjoy Christ as the lamb. You enjoy Christ in your home, and I enjoy Christ in my home. We all enjoy Christ wherever we are by ourselves. But when we come to the stage of the tabernacle being reared up among us and become the expression of Christ by enjoying Him more and more, we can be separated no longer. We must meet together, be joined together, and be built up together as one body. The forty-eight boards can never be separated. If they are separated, there can be no Ark among them as their content. There will be no place for the Ark as the testimony of Christ.

If we as a group of the Lord's people would go on to enjoy Christ in a more solid way than the redeeming lamb and the daily manna, if we would enjoy Him as the testimony of God, we must be built up together into one body as the tabernacle under the cover of the fullness of Christ. We must be one. It is at this stage that there must be something among the Lord's children in the way of oneness. This oneness is the tabernacle as the enlargement of the Ark. We can never go very far by ourselves, separately, singly, and individually. As such, we can receive Christ as our Redeemer, we can enjoy Him a little day by day as the manna, and we can even enjoy Him as the rock flowing with the living stream—indeed, as individuals we may enjoy Christ to this extent. But we can never go further than this and enjoy Christ in a more substantial way. We can never enjoy Him as the Ark of the Testimony of God, to say nothing about the land. Compare the Ark with the land. Consider how big the Ark is and how great the land is. There is a vast difference! The land is unsearchably great, unlimitedly great. The dimensions of the land are the length, the breadth, the height, and the depth of Christ! Yet if we cannot enjoy Christ as the Ark, it is certain we can never enjoy Him as the land. Not until we have been built up together with the people of God can we experience Christ as the Ark. We can never go on as a separate board.

In the Lord's building, all the numbers and dimensions always involve the figures five and three. This is true in all the building work of God throughout the Scriptures—in the ark of Noah, in the tabernacle, in the temple of Solomon, and in the temple recorded in Ezekiel. All the buildings contain the basic numbers of five and three. Why is this? Because the number three represents the Triune God in resurrection. And the number five is four, the number of the creature, plus one, the Creator; the creature plus the Creator becomes five. Man plus God becomes the God-man to take the responsibility. Therefore, the number five represents God and man, man and God, together as one to take the responsibility. In all the dimensions of the tabernacle we see these two numbers, five and three, signifying that the building of God is constituted of the Triune God in resurrection mingled with man. Now notice: the width of the boards is not three cubits, but one and a half cubits, or in other words, one half of three. This is most significant. It means that you are not a complete person; you are just a half. You must be joined to someone else. The Lord Jesus always sent out His disciples two by two. Saul and Barnabas were sent out together, not separately. Peter and John served together. It was always two by two. If you go by yourself, you are just half.

For example, when a brother comes into the meeting, we may say that he is just a half. When his wife follows a few moments later, there is the other half. When they sit together, you have the completion.

You must be deeply impressed that you are not a complete unit; you are only a half. You need to be coordinated in the Body. You can never simply be an individual. If you are individualistic, you will be spoiled.

It is rather difficult today to learn this lesson. Independence and individualism are stressed so much, and the Lord's children have been greatly influenced. But as the people of

God we can never be independent. If we are, we commit spiritual suicide.

Suppose my ear could say to my body, "I don't want to be joined to you. I want to be separated and independent." What would be the result of its independence? It would mean death to the ear. As a member of the Lord's Body, we must be united with others, not theoretically, but actually and practically. This ear must be united to a piece of skin, this piece of skin must be united to another part, and that part to still another, and so forth until you have the body. No part can be independent of the others. We must see this reality. It is not a nice thought or a teaching, but reality.

Let us seek to apply this principle to ourselves in a practical way. You are a member of the Body of Christ. Praise the Lord, we have been regenerated as members of His Body! Can you tell me, practically, to whom you are united? Can you name a brother or certain brothers with whom you are really one, with whom you are inwardly and practically one? Perhaps you will answer that you are united to the Head of the Body. But if my foot should answer in such a way, then it must be in the wrong position. It must be moved from the lower extremity of my body and joined directly to my head. But that is not God's arrangement. The Lord did not ask Peter to go with Him as a pair. God did not ask Paul to go with Christ as a pair. You must be united with someone other than Christ, some member other than the Head.

Wherever I go, if it is at all possible, I speak about this matter. But it is almost impossible to hear someone respond, "Brother, thank the Lord, I am definitely and practically united to a certain brother." If you live in Chicago, you cannot say that you are united to all the saints in Chicago. Practically, you are not. If you say this, it means that you are not united to anyone. We must be definitely united and practically built up with certain brothers and sisters.

Suppose we have the tabernacle here with its forty-eight boards and could ask the first board to whom it is united. It would answer without any hesitation that it is united to board number two, and we could clearly see that indeed it is. Then suppose we could ask board number two to whom it is united.

It would immediately answer that on one hand it is united to board number one and on the other hand to board number three—it could name definite boards to which it is united. All the boards could answer in such a way; therefore, they are all composed together to form God's dwelling place.

Brothers and sisters, if you can answer that you are definitely and practically related and united with certain others, it is a wonder of wonders. If so, we can really praise the Lord. The Lord will greatly bless your locality.

For the past thirty years, I can testify that by the Lord's grace I have been truly united with other brothers and sisters. If you were to ask me or if Satan were to ask me to whom I am united, I could immediately point to certain ones. I could say, "I am actually, definitely, and practically related to those very brothers and sisters in the Lord." Oh, this threatens the enemy! How he hates this! Wherever there are two or three who are really united together, it is a wonder and a testimony to the whole universe. Any two who have been really united can never be separated; they can never again act as individuals.

Oh, we must learn this lesson. This is the way to possess the good land. This is the way to enter into the all-inclusiveness of Christ. You must realize that you can never go on any further to enjoy Christ by yourself. At the most you can enjoy Him as the lamb, as the manna, and as the rock. That is all. Then you are finished. If you would enjoy Him more, you must be a board, one of many boards united together. How can you enjoy Christ as the Ark, the testimony of God, and the tabernacle as His enlargement if you are not united in the tabernacle? If you are not built into the tabernacle, you are cut off, you are kept out. You have nothing as far as the further and more solid enjoyment of Christ is concerned. When the tabernacle was reared up among the children of Israel, the Lord was not far away in heaven, nor was He in the wilderness; He was found in the tabernacle, in "the tent of meeting." In spiritual reality today, He is found in the practical building together of the saints in Him as His dwelling place. If you would enjoy Him as the Ark, you must be the boards united to be the tabernacle. He is not only a lamb; now He is the Ark.

He is not only a little piece of manna; now He is the Ark. And where is He as the Ark? He is in the tabernacle.

It is indeed regrettable that so many Christians have never come into the tabernacle. Twenty years ago they enjoyed Christ as little pieces of manna day by day, and today they still enjoy Him as such—nothing more. They are satisfied with this. And yet deeply within them, they are not satisfied. Twenty years ago they were truly satisfied when they enjoyed Christ as the manna, but not today. Twenty years ago they were so fresh; they were living in the newness of life in Christ. But today, if you meet them, they are full of oldness; their face is covered with wrinkles. They are still telling the same old story: "Oh, how good the Lord is to me day by day as the daily manna." But as they tell it, you may smell the oldness and see the wrinkles. Yes, they are enjoying Christ. It is quite good; but it is so old. It is not sweet anymore; it is not fresh.

Brothers and sisters, you and I must go on; we must make some advance in the enjoyment of Christ. We must have the newness of life, the newness of the Spirit, the freshness and the sweetness of an ever deepening and enriching enjoyment of Christ. Even if we remain here with the enjoyment of Christ as the Ark and after two years are still telling how we enjoy Christ in this way, you will sense the oldness. If for years to come we are continually speaking of Christ as the testimony, the explanation and the manifestation of God, you will certainly feel that we have become old. You will not smell a sweet savor but a stale odor. If the little children, two years of age, come to you, asking, "How are you?" you are really happy. The freshness and newness of life are in their words. But the very same words from the mouth of one twenty-two years of age are old. They lack the freshness, the newness.

We must make some advance. We must not be satisfied with our present state. There is so much more of Christ yet ahead of us to be enjoyed. But at this juncture, if you would enjoy Christ as the Ark of the Testimony of God, it is impossible as long as you are individual. You are finished; you are through. You must be subdued so that you will say, "Lord, here I am. I must be joined, I must be united, with some of Your children. Lord, lead me, point out to me the ones with whom I must be united. I am in this city; I am not in the New Jerusalem. Show me the ones in this locality, in this age, with whom I must be definitely and practically joined and related." Some may say that they would like to be joined to the apostle Paul or to Peter. But I am sorry, they are not here now. You must be joined to those whom the Lord has put here in your locality. You must be subdued. Perhaps the Lord will bring you together with a peculiar brother and say you must be joined to him. He will tell you that this is your dear brother, the one to whom you must be united. You will probably reply, "Lord, he is too peculiar. I just cannot take him!" But the Lord will answer, "He is the one. You have no other choice. Now go and take him." Learn the lesson. This is the greatest blessing, and this is the lesson we must learn in order to have the real building of the Lord.

I detest the present situation among the Lord's children. It seems that hardly one would submit himself to anyone. There is no submission, so there is no building. Whenever the tabernacle is raised up, the glory of God will immediately fill that place. Why is it that today there are so many groups of the Lord's children, but we never see the glory of God? It is because there is no building, no real unity, no real oneness. You may be continually meeting with the Lord's people yet never united to anyone. You are meeting, meeting, meeting, but you are an individualistic person—not merely an individual person but an individualistic person. There is no building between you and others, so the Lord can never be enjoyed or experienced in any further way. You are finished as far as the further experience of the Lord is concerned. I do not mean that you will perish, but that as far as the experience of the Lord is concerned, you can go no further until you are willing to be united with others. If you will be united with others, there will be a building between you and the Lord's children, and the tabernacle will come into existence in your locality. You will enjoy Christ in a much more solid way, as the Ark within the tabernacle.

Immediately after the tabernacle, as we have seen, we come to the priesthood. The priesthood is not the ministry or service of any individual person but the service of the Body.

No single person as an individual can be a priest—there is no such priesthood in the Old Testament. Priesthood does not mean individualism but a collective body. With yourself, individually speaking, the priesthood is nonexistent. By yourself, you can never say, "I am a priest." If you are united with your brothers and sisters, you may say, "We are priests." But if you are separated and become merely so many individuals, you can never say that you are the priests. Consider the Old Testament, the picture of the reality. Not one single person could act by himself, individually, as a priest. The priesthood is a body.

Then we come to the army. Could you by yourself ever constitute an army? Of course not. Neither could a number of separated individuals. An army must be constituted of a quantity of people formed and acting together as a unit. Some people today insist that wherever there are two or three meeting together in the Lord's name, it is sufficient. But are two or three an adequate number to form an army? For an army we need a host of people—the more the better.

If only two or three brothers and sisters invite me to speak to them, I will be glad to do it. If I do, however, after a short time I will be finished speaking; I will have no more to say. But if you give me a larger congregation—say, several hundreds or thousands—I can speak for hours without stopping.

Two or three is not enough. We must have a good number of brothers and sisters—the more the better. Never be satisfied with two or three. We must be joined with the brothers in the Lord; we must be joined with the people of God.

Why is the United States the first nation in the world today? Why is it the strongest nation? Because there are fifty united states. If there were only two or three states, for example, Missouri, Iowa, and Illinois, how weak the country would be! But there are fifty, all united under one government, so it is a mighty power.

Oh, how the subtle enemy wants to spoil the army of God! There are so many children of God, but not an army. It is really difficult in any place to find an army formed among the Lord's children; therefore, they are exceedingly weak. The United States is strong because it is united as one. But what about the Christians? Just consider the situation among the Lord's people in one city or area, to say nothing about the entire country and the world. It is a pity! It is a shame! There is no unity; there is no formation. Some people even oppose any kind of unity or formation. I am not speaking of a human formation or organization but a divine building, a real and practical unity among God's children. We hear many Christians in many places, saying, "Oh, as long as two or three of us can come together—two or three here, and two or three there—it is indeed good and quite sufficient." No, brothers and sisters! We are against this! We must be united with the Lord's children as an army. We must fight the battle, not just by two or three; it must be by a group of the Lord's children, a good number, an adequate number. I beg you in the Lord to pay the price for unity with the Lord's children. Give up all your opinions. As long as the Lord's people will recognize the all-inclusive Christ and be willing to have a real expression for Him, it is sufficient. We should pay any price for that. We should not insist upon anything but the all-inclusive Christ and the real expression for Him. Let us join with the Lord's children. Let us be formed as a strong army.

I am deeply burdened with this matter, so burdened that sometimes I am simply beside myself. I do not know anything but this; my whole mind and my entire being are given over to this matter. Oh, brothers and sisters, how we must cooperate with the Lord that He might recover these things! Let the Lord form us into an army in a practical way to fight the battle today for Him. Do not talk so nicely about the battle with Satan. The battle is immediately before you. This is the battle! Here is the battle! You must fight it, but not individually.

Before going to fight, we must be formed with others, and in order to be formed, we must be submissive. We must start by submitting ourselves to others. If we cannot be submissive, we can never be formed, we can never be built up together. Submission! There is a great need for submission among the Lord's children. Today is indeed a day of rebellion—the whole world is full of rebellion. In the family, in the school, in society, in the government, everyone is rebelling. You and I who are the children of God and who are being formed into an army to fight the battle for His kingdom must learn to submit. Contrary to the whole world course, we must learn the lesson of submission. We must submit ourselves to others and learn to say "yes." I do not mean that we should be a "yes-man," but that we must learn to say "yes" to others, not "no." It is so easy for people today to say "no." They are saying "no" to everybody and everything. It seems that many times, almost the first word the little children learn to say is "no." But we must not say "yes" in a false way, with the mouth but not with the heart. Our "yes" must be a "yes" with submission from a sincere heart. "Yes, brother!" "Yes, sister!" Submit yourself to them and learn to say "yes." Oh, may the Lord deliver us!

In most large cities there are thousands of Christians, but where is the army, where is the tabernacle, where is the priesthood? It is a pity. What can the Lord do? There is no unity, no oneness, no submission, no formation, no building up, no tabernacle, no priesthood, no army. There is no real dwelling place for the Lord on this earth. There is no real service to the Lord, because there is no priesthood. There is no real battle for the kingdom of God, because there is no real army. We are here for the recovery of these things.

We must be formed by submission into an army. The army is always under the priesthood, and the priesthood always accompanies the tabernacle. These three things always go together. Whenever there is a tabernacle, there is a group of priests. Then, surrounding the group of priests, is the army of the people. This is the picture of the reality which we must experience—the tabernacle, the priesthood, and the army. If there is no tabernacle, the priesthood is gone, and without the priesthood, there is no army of the people. The army depends upon the priesthood, and the priesthood is related to the tabernacle. And what is the tabernacle? The tabernacle is the place where the Lord's very presence is among His people. If there is no tabernacle, there is no presence of the Lord; the Lord's presence cannot be with us and cannot go with us. The Lord promised that His presence would go with us, but we must be clear where His presence dwells. His presence dwells in the tabernacle. If we have the tabernacle, we have His presence dwelling with us. If we do not have the tabernacle, we are finished; the presence of the Lord is gone.

The tabernacle, the priesthood, and the army! Brothers and sisters, do you have these among you? If not, you are not qualified; you are still short. You cannot go on to take possession of the land. We must be prepared with such qualifications. We must be in the full experience of the tabernacle, the priesthood, and the army. There is nothing individual about these matters. They all involve a collective body.

STRANGE FIRE

In order to maintain the tabernacle, the priesthood, and the army, besides individualism we must be exceedingly careful to avoid the following things; they will do great damage. The first is strange fire. We must never offer strange fire to God. What is strange fire? It is our natural enthusiasm; it is the fervency of our natural emotions, our natural zeal of heart. This inevitably brings in death. It kills our spiritual life and spoils the priesthood. The two sons of Aaron—Nadab and Abihu—offered strange fire, not out of ill will, but with a good intention. Yet it was strange fire. The Lord commanded that the fire to burn the incense be taken from the offering altar that the incense may be acceptable to Him. But they did not use the fire from the altar; they used strange fire. This means that their natural zeal, their natural enthusiasm, was not dealt with by the cross. This is an extremely vital matter. We must be dealt with by the cross. Our natural zeal must be put to death by the cross.

REBELLION

The second thing which we must avoid is rebellion against authority. Miriam and Aaron, the elder sister and elder brother of Moses, rebelled against Moses, who at that time was the authority. Yes, Moses did something which was not good— he married a Gentile woman. Undoubtedly he was wrong. That was his shortcoming, and Miriam and Aaron took it as the ground to oppose him. Nevertheless, regardless of what he had done, Miriam and Aaron must recognize authority, and

Moses was that authority. Regardless of everything, they must not rebel against authority. It is this very thing that spoils the oneness, the priesthood, and the formation of the army. Of course, as a leader we should be careful; we should not do anything typified by Moses' marrying of a Gentile woman. But on the other hand, and more important, you and I must learn never to be rebellious.

Perhaps in your city there is a local church, an expression of the Lord's Body, and in that church there are three or four leading brothers. You must realize that not one of us is one hundred percent perfect. Everyone has at least one shortcoming. Your eyes should not be so opened toward the elders; rather, they should be opened to the Lord. Do not set your eyes upon the elders to search them out. If you do, you are a rebellious one. You will spoil yourself.

Consider Miriam and Aaron. Were they right or wrong in what they said against Moses? Unquestionably, they were right, and Moses was wrong. Moses, as a servant of the Lord, gave the ground for their accusation. Yet when Miriam and Aaron took this ground and rebelled against authority, they brought upon themselves the judgment of God. Miriam was immediately gripped with leprosy, and although she was subsequently healed, Aaron and Miriam both died later in the wilderness.

In the past years I have seen many people who have become "leprous" as a result of their rebellion against the Lord's servants. Were the Lord's servants right? I would not say this. I admit that with each one there is at least one shortcoming. But the shortcomings of the Lord's servants are a test to us. They test where we are and what we have in our heart. What about your heart? It will be tested, not by the goodness of the Lord's servants but by their shortcomings.

Brothers and sisters, may you keep this word in your heart. This is a warning. I am well aware that the time will come when you will not be so happy with those who take the lead among you in the Lord. You will say, "What is this? Look what the leading brothers in the church have done!" It is a test to you. If you accuse them and rebel, you will become leprous.

The dirtiest one will not be them, but you. You will later fall, as Miriam and Aaron, by the wayside in the wilderness; you can never go on to share the all-inclusive, good land.

Later in the journey of the children of Israel, there was another rebellion, this time on a larger scale. Korah rose up with more than two hundred princes of the congregation to rebel against Moses and Aaron and brought death not only upon themselves but almost upon the whole congregation. Thousands of people died as a result of that rebellion. The unity was spoiled, the priesthood was spoiled, and the army of the Lord's people was spoiled. We need such a warning.

I believe many of you have a sincere heart toward the Lord for His testimony today. But we must remember that there is a rebellious nature within us. Some day, sooner or later, it will be tested. If we rebel, we will be spiritually cut off, and to a certain extent we will kill the testimony, the priesthood, and the army.

UNBELIEF

The third thing we must avoid is unbelief. It will surely kill us. You remember how those who spied out the land of Canaan brought back an evil report. On one hand, they said the land was exceptionally good, but on the other hand, they said that it was impossible to enter. The people there were giants, they said, and the cities fortified and great. They asserted that Israel could never conquer the land, and if they tried, they would be utterly defeated and devoured.

Many, many times the enemy, the evil one, speaks the very same things within us. He says, "Don't talk about the all-inclusive Christ. He is good and He is wonderful. But it is absolutely impossible for you to enter in." I am afraid that even while you have been reading these chapters, he has been whispering these things in your ear. "Don't ever think you can enter the good land; it is far beyond your ability. You will never make it." The little devil hidden in many of us is just waiting for an opportunity to inject his deadly poison. Never believe him. "The people are giants," he will tell you, "and the cities are fortified to heaven. You will be defeated, and you know it." Hebrews 3 tells us that this is an evil heart

of unbelief (v. 12). It is a heart occupied by the evil one, so it is
called an evil heart. We must ask the Lord to deliver our
heart from the evil one. We must pray, "Lord, I do want a good
heart, a heart full of faith. I am not able to enter the land, but
You are!" The One who is in us is greater than he that is in
the world. I cannot make it, but Christ can make it, and He is
in me. We must have faith in the power of His resurrection.
God is able to do exceeding abundantly above all that we ask
or think and all that we dream or imagine. God will do it; God
will make it. Let us follow the example of Joshua and Caleb.
They had hearts full of faith. They could tell the people, "Let
us go up at once and possess it; for we are well able to overcome it" (Num. 13:30).

Brothers and sisters, we must be very careful to avoid all
unbelief. I am deeply concerned that after reading so much
about the all-inclusive Christ, some of you will have an evil
heart of unbelief. Perhaps it will not be manifested now, but
you will later be tested. Perhaps while walking on the street
one day, you will say to yourself, "What! Who can ever do
that? Who can enjoy such an all-inclusive Christ? Not me! I'll
never be able!" This is an evil heart of unbelief. Call it by its
true name. Be careful! Be watchful! Be prayerful against it!

Indeed, in your natural strength you will never be able to
attain the good land. It is possible by resurrection power
alone. Only the power that raised Christ from the dead and
made Him the Head over all things can bring you in. But,
praise Him, this power is in us! This power is continually
being transmitted into us through the indwelling Holy Spirit.
Are we strong enough? Hallelujah, we are strong enough—not
in ourselves, but in Him; not in the flesh, but in the Spirit!
We will make it in the Spirit! Do you believe it, brothers and
sisters? Hallelujah! We must take it! Never be discouraged—
it is ours! Never think that you are too young. Yesterday
you were too young, but not today. Believe with full assurance
of faith! Christ is in you! You have been united with the
almighty God! Day by day His Spirit transmits into you all
that God is and all that God has. He will make it for you. As
long as you maintain your fellowship with Him, you will be
able to enter the land.

There will be some battles to be fought. But the battle is for the enemy; to you it will be a rest. The battle is a defeat to him but bread to you. Joshua and Caleb told the people, "Nor should you fear...for they are our bread" (14:9). The enemy will be our bread—we can go to eat them. If we do not engage in the battle, we will be hungry. Daily manna is not good enough; we must take and swallow up the enemy. The enemy will be our food, and to swallow him will be our satisfaction. Brothers and sisters, you and I must have living faith to go on, to take up the battle, and to swallow the enemy. The more you swallow, the more you will be satisfied. The defeated enemy is the best bread, the most tasteful bread. Let us cross the Jordan and take over Jericho. Let us devour the whole city as a tasteful dish. We will all be fully satisfied. Hallelujah! We need such a faith for such a battle.

WORLDLY CONNECTIONS

But, remember, the enemy is subtle. He will use the most subtle means to hinder and oppose us. Against Israel he used Balaam, the Gentile prophet, to cause them to join the world and commit fornication. The world will always spoil the army of God. We must be prayerful. We must be watchful for any worldly connections. When the enemy can do nothing else to spoil us, he will come in a very subtle way to deceive us and cause us to forge a union with something worldly. These things may not seem worldly to us; they may seem quite legitimate and proper. We can only escape by being in continual fellowship with the Lord. If we are caught by any union with the world, whether it be the secular or the religious world, we will be rendered powerless. May the Lord grant us grace to take this as a warning.

MURMURING

Furthermore, let us be watchful never to murmur against the Lord as did the children of Israel. We must always sing His praise. No matter how arduous the way, no matter what hardship you meet, always give praise to the Lord. This is the way of victory.

Remember these matters: never offer strange fire, never

rebel, abandon the evil heart of unbelief, be watchful for any union with worldly things, and never murmur against the Lord. If we do this, we will be ready to go on and take the land. We will be victorious!

Chapter Fourteen

ENTERING THE GOOD LAND

Scripture Reading: Josh. 1:1-6; 4:1-3, 8, 9; 5:2, 7-9, 10-12, 13-15; 6:1-11, 15, 16, 20; Col. 2:12; 3:1-5; Eph. 6:12, 13; 2 Cor. 10:3-5

Now we are ready to enter the good land. We have enjoyed the passover lamb in Egypt, we have left Egypt and crossed the Red Sea, we have enjoyed Christ as the daily manna and as the rock with the flowing stream, and we have experienced Christ as the Ark, the testimony of God. At this stage we are built together as His enlargement and His expression so that we become the tabernacle. We not only have the tabernacle, but we *are* the tabernacle. We are the expansion, the increase of Christ. We are built together, standing upon the solid basis of His redemption and covered over by the fullness of Christ. We are so strong and solid. We are one in Christ, who is the manifestation of God. Moreover, we know how to enjoy Christ time after time as all kinds of offerings. Therefore, we have the priesthood, and we are the priests. Furthermore, we have been formed under the priesthood to be the army, the divine army to fight the battle for that good land. We are prepared to fight and defeat the enemy. The host of Jehovah has been made ready by enjoying everything of Christ.

Oh, brothers and sisters, after we have passed through all these experiences, there is still something more wonderful ahead of us—the good land, the all-inclusiveness of Christ. We began with the little lamb, and we eventually come to the land of Canaan, the all-inclusive Christ. The land is still before us! We have enjoyed Christ, we have possessed Christ, and we have Christ—there is no doubt about it. And we are still enjoying Christ. Yet ahead of us is more of Christ. A

much greater Christ is waiting to be possessed, for the goal
God has set before us is the all-inclusive Christ. We must not
stop short of the goal.

BY TAKING THE WORD OF THE LORD

Suppose, then, we are ready to enter the land. We have
been formed into an army, and we are now the glorious,
divine, and heavenly host of Jehovah. What shall we do? First
of all, we must take the Word of the Lord. The Lord told
Joshua, "Now then arise, and cross over this Jordan, you and
all this people, into the land which I am giving to them, to the
children of Israel. Every place on which the sole of your foot
treads I have given to you" (Josh. 1:2-3). The Lord has promised it, but we must possess it. He has given it, but we must
experience it. It is our portion, but we must take it. We must
have the faith; we must have the confidence, the full assurance. It is not presently in our possession, but He will cause
us to take it; He will cause us to possess it. We must believe
Him and give Him our cooperation. Will we do it? Let us rise
up today and go forth to possess the land. Praise the Lord, it
is ours! Let us take it—not tomorrow, but today! Never say
"tomorrow." In unbelief, it is always tomorrow, tomorrow,
tomorrow. "Tomorrow" belongs to the devil! In faith there is
no tomorrow; it is always today. "Today" is ours! Brothers and
sisters, we must take it today! This is the first thing we must
do. We must stand on the Word of God. We must take the
Word of God and go on to possess the land.

BY REALIZING THAT WE HAVE BEEN BURIED

Secondly, we who are saved and have been enjoying Christ
must realize that we have been crucified on the cross. We are
dead, and we have been buried! We have an excellent hymn
that expresses this fact:

> Buried with Christ, and raised with Him too;
> What is there left for me to do?
>
> (*Hymns,* #483)

We have been buried with Christ; we have been finished! Do
you realize how big a word *buried* is? It would be good to

write it in large letters and hang it in your bedroom—
BURIED! Hang another in your dining room, another in your
living room, and another in your kitchen. Everywhere there is
a room—buried, buried, buried! I have been buried! I would
really be pleased to see a home decorated in this way. What a
rest it is to be buried! Could you have any better rest than
this? This is why the people of Israel were brought across the
Jordan in such a way. The Jordan was their burial.

When the children of Israel came out of Egypt, they
crossed the Red Sea, representing baptism. Now again, at the
Jordan, they passed through a body of water. It was a remembrance of the Red Sea. When we received Christ as our Savior,
the church baptized us—we were buried. But, regrettably,
not very long after, we forgot about it; we came out of the
grave. I do not say that we were raised up but that we came
out of the grave. Some even went struggling back to Egypt.
Now, because we have experienced Christ so much, because
we have Christ as the center of God's testimony and have
been built up into the tabernacle as the expression of Christ,
because we have the priesthood and the army of God and are
ready to take possession of the land, God tells us to make a
memorial, reminding us that we have been buried. From this
time forth, we must never forget that we have been buried.

The Red Sea and the Jordan represent the same thing—
the death of Christ. In the Red Sea the army of Egypt was
buried. Everything of this world and all the forces of this
world were buried there. Do you realize how many things and
how many people were buried with you when you were buried
in baptism? In the land from which I come, when a man died
and was to be buried, people buried with him all he had. Likewise, in the eyes of the Lord, when we were buried, all the
things we loved, all the things that comprised our world, were
buried with us. All the worldly army, all the worldly forces,
that formerly held us in bondage were buried. That is the
reality of the Red Sea. Now here at the river Jordan, God
wants to remind us once more. Not only the worldly forces were
buried, but we ourselves were buried too. We have been buried!

The crossing of the river Jordan is a beautiful and glorious
picture. The Ark with the priesthood entered the river first,

and there, in the heart of the river, the Ark with the priest-hood stayed. It is very meaningful. The Ark, as we have seen, is the Lord Christ, the testimony of God. Christ with the priest-hood went into the very heart of the river of death. Then all the people followed. All the people went down to the bottom of that river and passed that very spot. Then the Lord asked them to choose twelve people, one from every tribe of the twelve tribes of Israel. Each one took a stone from the place at the bottom of the river where the Ark stood and brought it to the other side of the Jordan, that is, to the good land. This signifies the resurrection. All those who entered the land of Canaan were those who were resurrected. They were new ones; they were not the old ones. They were the resurrected ones, not the natural ones. Only resurrected people can enter and possess the all-inclusive Christ; He is not for the natural man. We can enjoy Christ as the all-inclusive One only on the ground of resurrection. Brothers and sisters, we are resur-rected! We are buried and raised up! Now we are in Christ!

Then Joshua did something else to remind them of this fact. He took more stones, one for each of the tribes, and planted them at the very spot where the Ark stood. He buried them there as a memorial of the burial of the Israelites them-selves. In the eyes of God, all the children of Israel were buried in the river Jordan. This means that in the eyes of God we have all been buried in the death of Christ.

After all this was accomplished, the Ark with the priest-hood came out of the Jordan. After we were all put away, Christ emerged from death. Christ entered into death first, and Christ came out of death last; He was the first in and the last out; we were the last in but the first out. Christ com-pleted the death, and this death covers us all. We are all dead! We have all been buried with Christ! We can say, "Hallelujah, we have been buried! Now we are on the ground of resurrec-tion! Now we are in Canaan! Now we are in Christ, the good land!"

BY APPLYING THE DEATH OF CHRIST

Third, believing that we have been crucified with Christ and that we have been buried, we must apply this death to ourselves. Therefore, we must be circumcised. This is the application of the death of Christ to our flesh. If we realize that we are buried with Christ and raised with Christ, we must put our flesh to death; we must apply the death of Christ to our fleshly members. This is circumcision, and this is what we must practice day by day. We must daily take the ground that we are dead and buried and apply the death of Christ to our members. We not only need to apply His death to all our situation but also moment by moment to apply His death to our fleshly members and put them to death.

In the second chapter of Colossians we are told that we have been buried and raised with Christ and then in chapter three that our life is now hid with Christ in God. On this basis, we are then told in Colossians 3:5: "Put to death therefore your members which are on the earth." If we realize our burial and resurrection with Christ, we must apply His death to our fleshly members in a practical way by faith.

BY ENJOYING THE PRODUCE OF THE LAND

Fourth, immediately after applying the death of Christ to our members on the ground of being buried and resurrected with Him, we enjoy something of the life. We enjoy the produce of the land, the all-inclusive Christ. The manna stops, and the produce of the land takes its place. The large Christ replaces the little Christ. Before this, we were continually enjoying a little Christ—the manna. But by this time, the little Christ has ceased. Now we are tasting the greater, the richer, the fuller Christ; now we are enjoying the land, the all-inclusive Christ.

Brothers and sisters, are you now enjoying the manna, or are you now enjoying the land? What are you enjoying today? Undoubtedly, we are all enjoying Christ, but what kind of Christ? Perhaps there are some who are enjoying Christ only as the lamb of the passover. Most of us, probably, are enjoying Him only as the daily manna. But the produce of the land is much better than manna. What is your experience? Perhaps some of you would say that it is very difficult to answer. Sometimes you enjoy Christ as the manna, and sometimes, it seems, you enjoy Christ as the produce of the land. Whether or not you enjoy Him as the produce of the land depends very much on your burial. How much have you realized that you have been buried and that you are now on the ground of resurrection?

Let me illustrate. Suppose that early this morning I met a certain person who is extremely peculiar. This particular person always causes me to experience the resurrection life. The Lord has created this person and in His sovereign wisdom has brought him to me. He knows why I need him. In order to deal with him I need the very power of resurrection day by day. Suppose that early this morning this person acted very strangely and greatly disturbed me. I was exceedingly unhappy with him and my anger was aroused. Then, returning to my room, I felt condemned in my conscience and made confession to the Lord. I said, "Lord, forgive me! I failed; I have been defeated. But, I praise You, Lord, I am cleansed by Your precious blood!" After confessing and being forgiven, I was nourished; I enjoyed something of Christ. What kind of enjoyment was this? It was the enjoyment of Christ as a little bit of manna. I enjoyed the manna.

Now suppose that another day this same person troubled me again, and I was disturbed by him. But this time I took the ground of resurrection. I said, "Lord, I am resurrected! On the ground of resurrection, I exercise my spirit to put my members to death." Then instead of being angry with him, I was so happy in the Lord. I could say, "Hallelujah! Praise You, Lord, for my dear, peculiar brother!" I applied the Lord's death to my members which are always angry with others, and I gained a fresh experience and enjoyment of Christ. What kind of experience was this? This experience was quite different from that of Christ as the manna. This was an experience of Christ as the produce of the good land. You see, both were experiences of Christ, but Christ in different aspects. In the first way I enjoyed Christ as the little manna, and in the second way as the rich produce of the land.

BY FIGHTING THE BATTLE

Fifth, we not only need to remember that we have been buried, that we are on the ground of resurrection, and that we must apply the Lord's death to our members in a practical way, but we must also remember that there are evil powers in the heavenlies. We must fight the battle with the enemy. Though we are enjoying a portion of the all-inclusive Christ, yet the enemy and his evil forces in the heavenlies are still usurping and occupying the land. You and I have to fight the battle to take possession of the entire land. Brothers and sisters, as soon as we enjoy Christ in such a way, we realize in our spirit the reality of the evil forces in the heavenlies. These evil forces are veiling the all-inclusiveness of Christ from the Lord's children. Very few of the Lord's people can realize the all-inclusiveness of Christ simply because of the accusations of the evil powers in the heavenlies. To this very day, the evil forces are still veiling the all-inclusiveness of Christ. Therefore, we must fight the battle. There is an exceedingly real spiritual warfare in which we must engage. By enjoying something of the all-inclusive Christ, we will be burdened for this fighting; we will be burdened for this battle. That is why we have been formed as an army. The conflict is before us.

It is at this stage that we are given the vision of the Lord Christ as the prince, the glorious captain, of the host of Jehovah. He will take the lead in the army; He will go before us; He will fight the battle for us. We need such a vision. How could Joshua receive this vision? It was simply because he was exceedingly burdened for the battle before him. Immediately after he and the people of Israel enjoyed the produce of the good land, he realized that before them lay the enemy and the stronghold of Jericho. Joshua had a clear view of the situation, and he was burdened for the battle. I believe that because of this he went to the Lord in prayer, and at that time the Lord revealed Himself to Joshua as the prince of the host of God. Joshua received such a vision, and thereby the faith and assurance that the Lord was with him. He knew then without a shadow of doubt that the Lord Himself as the prince of the army of God was going before him. We too need such an assurance.

Some can testify from their own experience that immediately after enjoying something of the all-inclusiveness of Christ they have realized the need of spiritual warfare. They have seen that the enemy and his evil powers in the heavenlies are still usurping the good land of the all-inclusive Christ and veiling it from the Lord's children. Who will fight the battle to uncover the land? If we enjoy Christ in such a way, we will spontaneously go to the Lord with a burden for the battle. It is then that He will give us a vision of Himself as the captain. He will show us that He is at the head of the army, and He will go before us to fight the battle. We can then go forward with full assurance.

HOW TO FIGHT THE BATTLE

Now we come to the last step. How shall we fight the battle? This is certainly not a battle fought with carnal weapons. Our weapons for this battle, figuratively speaking, are *rams' horns*. We go to a battle, but we go with instruments of peace; we go with rams' horns. Rams' horns are a symbol of fighting a warfare with peaceful weapons. They are not swords made of iron; they are rams' horns. They cannot kill; they are utterly peaceful. But they are weapons for battle. They are trumpets to be blown, declaring and proclaiming the gospel of peace. This is the weapon we must use to fight the spiritual warfare. We fight by proclaiming Christ!

In what way were the trumpets blown and the battle executed? It was indeed strange. Part of the army went before, followed by seven priests with the Ark. Bringing up the rear, was another part of the army. In other words, before and behind was the army, and in the midst was the Ark with the priests blowing the rams' horns. They all marched around the stronghold of Jericho, the priests blowing the trumpets of rams' horns as they went. It was a glorious picture. The people in the city were in dread of them and shut the gates of the city from within and without. None went out and none came in.

Day by day the army of God, six hundred thousand strong, marched around the city, blowing the rams' horns. First came one division, then the priests blowing the trumpets, then the Ark, and then the remainder of the army at the rear. This was the way they pressed the battle. There were probably some people in Jericho who laughed and scorned them. They had never seen such an unworldly performance. Once a day they compassed the city, day after day for six days repeating the same procedure. When the seventh day came, as they were instructed, they compassed the city seven times.

We must notice here that Joshua commanded the people, saying, "You shall not shout, nor let your voice be heard, nor let a word go forth from your mouth, until the day I say to you, Shout! Then you shall shout" (Josh. 6:10). Not until they heard the long blast of the rams' horns at the end of the final circuit were the people to shout—before that time they were to keep silence. What is the meaning of this? It means that if we are going to testify the victorious Christ, there are many times when we must be silent; we must let the priesthood blow the trumpet. We need the priesthood, and by now you understand what we mean by the priesthood. We must not speak lightly. Do not say, "Oh, we are on the church ground! Oh, we are the local church! We are this, and we are that!" If you say these things lightly, there is no priesthood. We must let the priesthood blow the trumpet and give the sound. There must be no other voice. Then when the time comes, the time appointed by the Lord, you and I must shout. We must pray and praise the Lord with a loud voice, and the enemy will fall before us. This is the way for us to fight the battle.

Is such a battle a kind of labor or a form of enjoyment? Indeed, it is not a labor but an enjoyment. It is even a rest and satisfaction. It is a war, it is a fight, it is a battle, and yet it is an enjoyment, a rest, and a satisfaction. It is in this way that we possess the all-inclusiveness of Christ.

But we must remember well that you and I as separated individuals can never do it. We must always maintain the ground as an army. The all-inclusive Christ can never be apprehended by ourselves as individuals. We can only apprehend the breadth, the length, the height, and the depth of the all-inclusive Christ with all the saints. To take possession of the good land, we must be formed and united together with the saints as the army of God.

We must also remember that our enemies are not flesh and blood; they are not people. They are the spiritual forces, the principalities, the powers in the heavenlies. There are many people who are against us and opposing us, but they are not our enemies. Our enemies are the evil forces who rule over them, the evil powers who are behind them. We are not fighting with people, but with the evil forces behind the people. If we are faithful with the Lord to take the ground of resurrection and be formed into an army to fight the battle for Him, we must be ready for many evil reports to be spread concerning us. We must be prepared for considerable opposition. All the people of Jericho will talk about the people of Israel. But, praise the Lord, whenever we hear these reports, we may rejoice, for they are signs that we will win. They are signs that the enemy is in fear and his defeat is inevitable. Jericho will certainly fall before us. Hallelujah! I am really fearful wherever I go if no one talks about me and there are no evil reports. But I am so happy if there are rumors, criticisms, and people talking. The more I hear of this, the more I come back to the Lord and praise Him: "Here are the signs, Lord; here are the signs that the battle will be won!" The foolish talking, the absurd rumors, the evil reports—we should not be afraid of them. They are all signals that the victory is ours. Praise the Lord!

Our enemy is not on this earth, but in the heavenly places. Hence, we should not use weapons of flesh. We should not argue with people; we should not come down to their level and engage in their tactics. No. Our weapons are spiritual. What are they? They are the trumpets of rams' horns. Let us blow the trumpets; let us blow the rams' horns. Let us declare the victory of the cross, the victory of the victorious One. We must proclaim Christ—the Christ we enjoy, the Christ who is the Conqueror over every foe. This is our weapon—we know nothing else. This is the way to possess the all-inclusiveness of Christ. This is the way to take the good land in faithfulness, in rest, and in enjoyment.

City by city and place by place, we must take possession of the all-inclusiveness of Christ. But be at peace and rest well. Do not worry—the Lord will fight the battle. The battle is not ours but the Lord's. What we must do is just to blow the trumpet. Do not speak lightly. At the right time we will praise and shout, and the walls of Jericho will fall. Its doom is sealed. We will be victorious, and we will take over.

Brothers and sisters, this is the way. The victory is ours! Take the ground of resurrection, remembering that you are buried; apply the death of Christ to all your earthly members; enjoy Christ with the saints in the way of all-inclusiveness and declare and testify in faith all that the Lord is. Then the enemy will be utterly defeated and his stronghold cast down. We will defeat the enemy and take the land peacefully with rest and satisfaction. The enemy will be our bread; to engage in such a warfare will be our full satisfaction. The battle is the Lord's. There is nothing left for us to do but proclaim and enjoy the victory.

> Hallelujah! Christ is Victor,
> Tell with ev'ry breath,
> That the Savior still is conqu'ror
> Over sin and death.
>
> Hallelujah! Christ is Victor,
> Tell where'er you go,
> That the Lord is still the conqu'ror,
> Over every foe.
>
> Hallelujah! Christ is Victor,
> Pain and sickness flee,
> When we plead the mighty victory
> Won on Calvary.
>
> Hallelujah! Christ is Victor,
> Therefore do and dare;
> Go wherever Jesus sends you
> In prevailing prayer.
>
> Hallelujah! Christ is Victor,
> No defeat nor fear
> Evermore must dim thy vision!
> Christ the way will clear.
>
> Hallelujah! Christ is Victor,
> Soon His voice shall ring,
> "Come ye conquerors, come up hither,
> Join thy conquering King."

> (*Hymns*, #890)

CHAPTER FIFTEEN

LIFE IN THE LAND

Scripture Reading: Deut. 12:1-18, 20-21, 26-27; 14:22-23; 16:16-17

Suppose that we have already taken possession of the land. We have entered into it, we have defeated and subdued all the enemies, and we are living in it. Now we must discover what manner of life we should have in the land.

We have seen firstly something about the land. The land is good; it is exceedingly good. It is good firstly in its spaciousness, secondly in its transcendency, and thirdly in its riches—three items. We have seen the details of its riches: it is rich in waters, in all kinds of food, both vegetable and animal, and in minerals. We have also been greatly occupied with the way to enter and possess the land, from the lamb of the passover through many more experiences of Christ. Now we are in this wonderful land; we are in the all-inclusive Christ. What kind of life should we have in this good land? The book of Deuteronomy deals with this.

By the time Moses, the servant of the Lord, wrote the book of Deuteronomy, everything was ready for the people of Israel to enter into the land. They had the tabernacle with the Ark, they had the priestly service, and they were coordinated and formed into an army. All things were in readiness; the next step was to enter in. But Moses realized that he was not called by the Lord to lead the people into the land. It was he who brought them to this stage of full preparedness, but he himself could not enter into the land with them. The Lord told him that he must leave. At that moment, the heart of this servant of the Lord went out in love to the people of the Lord. He was very much concerned about their future, especially regarding their life after they took possession of the land. Therefore, with such love and concern, he did his best to instruct them regarding the manner of life they should live after they possessed the land. He was just like an elderly father urging words of wisdom and loving counsel upon his maturing children. His speech to them was full of admonitions to be careful regarding the life they would live in the land promised by the Lord to their fathers; otherwise, they would lose it. This was the burden he discharged to them and recorded in this book.

The book of Deuteronomy precedes the book of Joshua, but the contents of Deuteronomy deal with that which follows Joshua. In the order of the books, it is first, but in the matters with which it deals, it is subsequent. Joshua deals with the possession of the land—crossing the river, fighting the battle, entering the land, and wresting it from the usurping enemy. Deuteronomy, however, deals with the life we should have in the land after it has been possessed. In other words, it shows us the life we should live in order to enjoy what we have possessed. We have entered the land and taken possession of it; now we must learn how to enjoy it and live within it. We must not only know how to take possession of the all-inclusiveness of Christ, but also after possessing Him how to live a life in the eyes of God that will enable us to enjoy Him. This is the message of the book of Deuteronomy.

LABORING ON CHRIST

What then is the life we need to enjoy the good land? It is a life first of all of laboring upon Christ. It is a life of making Christ our industry.

So much is said today about industry. People study many subjects for industry, they go into business for industry, and cities are planned for industry. Practically everything today is for industry. Nations are even competing with each other in the matter of industrial growth. There are many kinds of industries in the world, but we who are the Lord's people living in the all-inclusive Christ should have one industry—Christ. Christ is our industry. We must labor upon Him.

Many today are students of science or engineering. Day by day they are delving into these matters and working upon them. They spend many hours of laborious study, experimentation, and even practice in these fields. But, please tell me, as a Christian, born of God, enlightened by the Holy Spirit, and strengthened daily by resurrection power in your inner man, on what are you laboring? In other words, what is your business?

Wherever I go, I never like to tell people that I am a preacher. It may sound strange, but I feel shameful to make myself known to others in such a way. And I do not like to let people know that I am a so-called minister. It is really difficult for me to tell people my business. Many times when I am traveling by air or by train, someone sits beside me and asks me concerning my occupation. Sometimes I startle them by replying: "I am working on Christ! Christ is my job!" When they ask me what firm I am working for, I sometimes answer, "My firm is Christ Incorporated!" Then they usually ask what I mean by "Christ Incorporated." I can only tell them that day by day I am working on Christ and that Christ Himself is my very business.

You who are students must realize and experience even while studying that you are working upon Christ. Christ is your industry. You who are truck drivers must realize that truck driving is not your real occupation; your real business is Christ; you must be working on Him continually. You who are housewives must know that your real work is not caring for your home and your family, but *Christ*! Are you working on Christ all the time? Are you seeking to enjoy Him and experience Him in every situation?

The life after the possession of the good land is a life of laboring upon Christ. It is a life of making Christ our industry and producing Him in mass production. We are working for "Christ Incorporated," and day by day we are producing Christ. Many farmers are fruit growers and fruit producers. We are Christ growers and Christ producers. We are working diligently day and night on the farm of Christ. Yet we are working happily, and our work is such a rest to us.

Consider the people of Israel after they occupied the good

land and all their enemies were subdued. What did they do? They simply labored on the land. They tilled the ground, sowed the seed, watered the plants, nurtured the vines, and pruned the trees. These were all necessary tasks for the enjoyment of that piece of land. It is a picture of how we must work diligently upon Christ that we may enjoy His all-inclusive riches. This is our business. Christ is our industry. We must work on Christ to produce His riches. We have seen how rich that good land is in so many aspects, but without laboring upon it, how could its riches be brought forth and abundantly produced? To have this rich Christ is one thing, but to continually labor upon Him is another.

What about today's Christianity? Is it rich, or is it poor? We must confess that it is indeed poor. Christ is rich beyond measure, but the church today is groveling in poverty. Why? It is because the Lord's children today are indolent. They will not exert themselves to labor upon Christ. Read the Proverbs written by that wise man, King Solomon. "How long, sluggard, will you lie there? / When will you arise from your sleep? / A little sleep, a little slumber, / A little folding of the hands to rest, / And your poverty will come upon you like a robber" (Prov. 6:9-11). How is it that America today is so rich? God indeed gave America an exceedingly rich land. But this is not the whole story. Many Americans have worked diligently upon this land to produce its riches, to bring forth its abundant wealth. We have to work; we cannot be lazy. What about most Christians today? They are too busy with their worldly industries, and they are too lazy in working upon Christ.

We must till our spiritual ground; we must sow the spiritual seed; we must water the spiritual plants—all the time. We cannot rely upon others to do it for us; we must do it ourselves, or it will never be done. Sisters, have you pray-read the Word this morning? Brothers, how many times have you contacted the Lord today? This is the situation. We do not cultivate Christ. We have a very rich land, but we do not work on it, so there is no produce. We are indeed rich in resource but poor in produce.

The Lord told His people that they must come together to worship Him at least three times a year: at the time of the

Passover, at the time of Pentecost, and at the Feast of Tabernacles. And He told them that whenever they come together,
they should in no wise come with their hands empty. They
must bring something in their hands to Him, something of
the produce of the good land. If they were lazy and did not
work on the land, not only would they be unable to bring anything to the Lord, but they would have nothing to satisfy
themselves; they would be hungry.

Brothers and sisters, we must realize that whenever we
come to the meetings, whenever we come to worship the Lord,
we should not come with our hands empty. We must come with
our hands full of the produce of Christ. We have to labor upon
Christ day by day so that we produce Him in mass production. We need more than just a little of Christ to satisfy our
own needs. We must produce enough of Him so that there will
be a surplus remaining for others, for the poor and for the
needy: "You must open your hand to your brother, to the poor
one with you and to the needy one with you in your land" (Deut.
15:11). There must also be a surplus to meet the needs of the
priests and the Levites: "This shall be the priests' rightful due
from the people, from those who offer a sacrifice, whether an
ox or a sheep: They shall give the priest the shoulder...You
shall give him the firstfruits of your grain, of your new wine,
and of your fresh oil, and the first shearing of your sheep"
(18:3-4). And above all, the best of the surplus must be
reserved for the Lord: "Then to the place where Jehovah your
God will choose to cause His name to dwell, there you shall
bring all that I am commanding you, your burnt offerings and
your sacrifices, your tithes and the heave offering of your
hand and all your choice vows which you vow to Jehovah"
(12:11). When they harvested the field, they were to reserve
the firstfruits for the Lord. When the cattle were brought
forth, the firstborn were for the Lord. We must labor diligently, not only to bring forth enough to satisfy our own needs
but also to acquire a surplus to meet the needs of others, with
the best reserved for the Lord. Then we will be acceptable
to the Lord, and He will be pleased with us.

This is the life in the good land. It is a life in which we are
continually laboring upon Christ, in which we are producing

Him in a mass way. We are reaping so much of Christ that we are fully satisfied, and beyond that we have a surplus to share with others and to worship God. To worship God with Christ does not mean to worship Him individually but to worship Him collectively with all the children of God by enjoying Christ with one another and with God. When you come, you bring something of Christ. When he comes, he brings something of Christ. Everyone brings a portion of Christ from his laboring upon Him, and there is a rich enjoyment of Christ, not only by all the saints but most of all by God, to whom the best is offered.

HOW TO LABOR ON CHRIST

We have seen briefly our need to work upon Christ and make Christ our industry. I believe we are clear regarding this matter, but I am afraid it may be merely a doctrine to many. How can we apply it in a practical way? What must we do to work on Christ daily?

Let me illustrate. Every morning you need to pray: "Lord, I consecrate myself once more to You, not to work for You but to enjoy You." You must consecrate yourself sincerely to the Lord for the simple purpose of enjoying and experiencing Him— nothing more. From the moment you awake in the morning you need to say, "Lord, here I am. I give myself to enjoy You. Grant me through the entire day, from this moment on, to experience and apply You in every situation. I am not asking for anything tomorrow. I am asking for grace to enjoy You today. Show me how to till the ground, sow the seed, and water the plants of the Lord." Moment by moment through the whole day you will maintain your communion with the Lord. You will live practically in the Lord, laboring upon Him, applying Him, and enjoying Him. If you do this, consider how fruitful and how beautiful your "farm" will be. The farm of Christ in your daily life will be full of produce. When the Lord's Day comes and you go to worship the Lord with the saints, you will be able to say, "I am going now to see my God; I am going to worship my Lord. I will not go with empty hands but with hands full of Christ. I have a surplus, and in my right hand is the best part reserved for my dear Lord."

When you come to the meeting, a brother may approach you, saying, "I am having a certain problem. Could you help me?" You can have a little fellowship with him and pass on some of your surplus of Christ. You can give him a little of the produce from the Christ upon whom you have been laboring, the Christ whom you have been enjoying day by day. You have been abundantly satisfied with Him, and you have something over to share with the brothers and sisters. When the meeting begins, you are well prepared to offer your prayers and praises to the Lord from your reserve for Him. This is the best of your surplus, and with the saints you joyfully render it to the Lord for His enjoyment and satisfaction. You have reaped enough of Christ for yourself, for the needy ones, and for the Lord. You have furthermore put aside a considerable portion which will stand you in good stead in future days.

If we are rich with Christ, we must necessarily be rich with work, rich with industry. In Christ we cannot be lazy. We must let God enjoy Christ with us and at the same time with others. If you do this, I do this, and we all do this, how wonderful the meetings will be when we come together to worship the Lord! I will share with you, and you will share with me. You will give me something of the Lord, and I will give you something in exchange. There will be every kind of sharing and mutual enjoyment. And the Lord will have His full portion.

EXHIBITING CHRIST

In the world today there are many exhibitions and fairs. At certain times people from all over certain areas and districts and sometimes from throughout the entire world bring their products together for exhibition. This is just what we are doing when we come together to worship God. We are meeting together to have an exhibition of Christ, not just the Christ God gave us but the Christ we have produced, the Christ upon whom we have labored and whom we have experienced. That is the Christ whom we all come together to exhibit. Brothers and sisters, this is what all our meetings should be—an exhibition, a fair, in which all sorts of the produce of Christ are displayed.

Consider again the people of Israel. At the time of the

feast of tabernacles, so many from all over the land came together to their center, Jerusalem. All brought with them some of their produce—some fruit, some vegetables, some cattle, and many other things. If we could be there at that time and witness the occasion, we would marvel at the riches of the land. We would behold the abundance of the produce heaped here and there—beautiful, ripened, and in many colors—with the sheep and the cattle on every hand. Everything was put together and mutually enjoyed in the presence of Jehovah, God too having His own portion.

Brothers and sisters, the church life is simply this. It is all the saints enjoying Christ before God and mutually with God. They are enjoying the Christ they produce. Day by day they are working on Christ; day by day they are producing Christ. Then on a certain day appointed by the Lord they come together. Not only are their hands full, but even upon their shoulders, figuratively speaking, they are bearing Christ. They are rejoicing in the abundance of their harvest and in all the riches they have reaped from that "good land" in which they are living. They are not coming empty handed with wrinkled and smileless faces. They are not sleeping in the pews while a poor minister occupies the platform. How miserable is this kind of situation! This is certainly not the worship of the Lord's people. The worship of His people is when everyone is full of Christ, radiant with Christ, and exhibiting the Christ upon whom they have labored and whom they have produced. One brother could say, "Here is the Christ whom I have labored upon and produced today. He is so rich and abundant to me in this aspect and in that aspect." A sister could testify, "Praise the Lord, I have experienced the very patience and kindness of Christ in my difficult home situation. He is so sweet and real to me in this way." This is her produce of Christ. Everyone exhibits the Christ whom they have reaped. What a worship to God, what an edification to the saints, and what a shame to the enemy! This kind of meeting is a great embarrassment to the principalities and powers in the heavenly places. The evil forces beholding it are put to shame that Christ is such a Christ. Brothers and sisters, do you have meetings like this in your locality?

I fear that the enemy today is laughing and the wicked forces in the heavenlies are mocking our Christian meetings. But we can turn the tables on them by enjoying the all-inclusive Christ, by laboring diligently upon Him day after day, and by bringing our abundant produce of Him together to share with God and with all the saints. If we do this, the enemy and his hosts will tremble with rage and shame.

This is the life after the possession of the good land. It is a life of working on Christ, producing Christ, enjoying Christ, sharing Christ with others, and offering Christ to God that He may enjoy Him with us. This kind of enjoyment and sharing is an exhibition of Christ to the entire universe. It is a worship to God and a shame to the enemy. Every time after such a worship, not one of the Lord's children will be poor. Everyone will be rich, everyone will be satisfied, and everyone will go from "Jerusalem" rejoicing. At the conclusion of such a meeting all the brothers and sisters will be richly and abundantly nourished. They came with a surplus, and they leave with a greater surplus. Everything of the life in the land is Christ, but it is a Christ related to us. It is not merely an objective Christ but a very subjective Christ. It is a Christ who is labored upon by us, a Christ who is produced by us, a Christ who is enjoyed by us, a Christ who is shared with others and offered to God by us.

TWO WAYS OF ENJOYING CHRIST

According to the book of Deuteronomy there are two ways set forth for enjoying Christ. One could be called the personal, individual way, and the other the collective way. For instance, as far as the grain—the wheat and the barley—was concerned, all the people of Israel at any time and in any place could enjoy it. This is one way of enjoying the produce of the land. But some of the grain could not be enjoyed individually and separately. The tithe and firstfruits of the grain together with the tithes and firstfruits of all their harvest must be preserved and on a certain day brought to the priests chosen by God. They must be brought to the place where God's habitation was located, the place where He put His name. At that place in the presence of God, these things were to be enjoyed together with all the children of God and with God Himself. This was the collective worship.

These two ways applied also to the cattle. If they desired to eat the meat of the flock or of the herd, they could slay the animals in any place and enjoy them. But they could not eat the firstborn; they could not eat the tithe. That must be kept and brought to the priest at the place where the Lord put His name, where the Lord made His habitation and where the Lord's children met. On one hand, they could enjoy something of the riches and fullness of the good land in any place. Whenever and wherever they felt the need, they could do so. But on the other hand, there was a portion for which they had no choice and no liberty. They must take it to the place chosen by God to enjoy it together with His children. Thus, there were these two ways: the individual way and the collective way.

Now let us apply these principles. We as Christians may enjoy Christ anytime and anywhere by ourselves. But if we would enjoy Christ in a collective way with the Lord's children, we have no choice; there is only one place to which we can go. To enjoy Him separately and individually is permissible anywhere—for this we have full liberty. But if we would enjoy Christ with the Lord's people as worship to God, we must go to the very place chosen by God. This is an extremely vital matter, for it preserves the unity of the Lord's children.

This principle is entirely contrary to the situation which prevails in today's Christianity. How much confusion, complication, and division have been created by the violation of it! Consider the children of Israel. For generation after generation, through century after century, there was no division among them, for they had only one center for their worship. No one dared establish another. There was only one location for them to gather, one place for them to worship—the place which Jehovah chose out of all their tribes to put His name and His habitation. In all the land of Israel, Jerusalem was unique. It was the place appointed by the Lord to which all the people must come for collective worship to Him.

Let us read the Word of the Lord:
> Deuteronomy 12:5-8: To the place which Jehovah
> your God will choose out of all your tribes to put
> His name, to His habitation, shall you seek, and
> there shall you go. And there you shall bring your
> burnt offerings and your sacrifices and your tithes
> and the heave offering of your hand and your vows
> and your freewill offerings and the firstborn of
> your herd and of your flock; and there you shall eat
> before Jehovah your God...You shall not do accord-
> ing to all that we do here today, each man doing all
> that is right in his own eyes.

When we come into that land which is the all-inclusive Christ,
we can no longer do what is right in our own eyes. We cannot
meet with the Lord's children for corporate worship in the
places we choose. We must go to the place which the Lord has
chosen, to that one center, that one ground of unity.* How
contrary is today's situation! If there are nine or ten brothers
in a certain place, it is so easy for them to say, "Come, let us
form a new church." And if two or three do not agree, they will
say, "All right, you go and form your church." And they will.
Just in one locality it is rather difficult to count how many
so-called churches there are. In Christianity today everyone
acts as if he has the right to choose according to his own
desire. The saying is popular and current, "Attend the church
of your choice." I would like to shout at the top of my voice to
all the Lord's children, *"You have no choice!"* On one hand, you
have full liberty to enjoy Christ by yourself wherever you are,
but when you gather with the Lord's children to worship Him
you have lost your liberty. The place where the Lord's children gather must be the very place appointed by the Lord
Himself. We must go to that place.

If you were an Israelite in the Old Testament times, you
could not say to David or Solomon, "I am not happy with you.
If you worship at Jerusalem, I will go to Bethlehem. I will set
up another center of worship at Bethlehem." But this is just

---

*See chapter 4 of *Further Talks on the Church Life* by Watchman
Nee, published by Living Stream Ministry.

what people are doing today. "We do not want to be where you are. If you are meeting on First Street, we will start a meeting on Second Street." They even seek to justify what they are doing by quoting Matthew 18:20: "Where two or three are gathered together into My name, there am I in their midst." They say, "What we are doing is quite scriptural. We are two or three meeting in the name of the Lord, and we are meeting on the ground of Christ." A few months after beginning this meeting, some brothers in their midst will not feel happy there and will leave to set up yet another meeting. They will say, "If you can set up a meeting on Second Street, we can set up a meeting on Third Street." What confusion this is! In such a situation, there is no limitation, there is no rule, and the divisions will be endless.

We must meet together with the children of God on the common ground of unity. You cannot say that this ground is too legal. We must be legal in such a way. You and I have to be limited by the rule of God. We have no right to set up another center for worship—it will only create a division among the Lord's children. The only ground we can take and stand upon is the ground of unity. We can enjoy Christ anywhere by ourselves, but we absolutely cannot set up a meeting anywhere to enjoy Christ with other brothers and sisters as worship to God. Not one of us has any right to do this. We must all go to the very place which the Lord has appointed, where He has set His name and where His habitation is. In the whole universe the Lord's Body, the Lord's dwelling place, is only one; therefore, in every place there should only be one expression of it. This is a basic rule.

Brothers and sisters, read the book of Deuteronomy. The two rules for enjoying Christ in the land are clearly set forth. One pertains to your own personal enjoyment of the produce of the good land. You can do it anywhere and everywhere, whenever and wherever you please. The other rule is that if you would enjoy the produce of the good land together with the Lord's people before God as worship, you have no choice, you have no right to follow your own inclinations and do what is right in your eyes. You must give up your own thoughts and say in fear and trembling, "Lord, where is the place that You have chosen? Let me know where You have put Your name, where Your habitation is. I will go there." There you can enjoy Christ with all God's children and with God Himself in His very presence.

If you would do this, I can assure you, you will be most pleasing to God. If otherwise, you will be against Him by increasing the division among His children. You must be exceedingly careful. I beg you to hearken to these words.

Christ is so full, so rich, and so living! We can enjoy Him anytime and all the time. It is not only permissible but proper that we seek to enjoy Him wherever we are. But we must remember the basic and strict rule, that if we would enjoy Him with the Lord's people before God as worship, we cannot do as we like. We must be in fear and trembling in this matter!

Brothers and sisters, are you meeting now with God's children in the place which He has appointed, in the place where He has put His name? I would advise you to stop and look to the Lord. Seek the Lord. Ask Him to show you the place He has chosen and tell Him you will go to that place. This is the right way for us to solve the problem of division among the Lord's people today. There is no other way. May He be merciful to us.

The life in the land is a life full of the enjoyment of Christ, both personally and collectively with the Lord's people. May we be diligent to labor upon Him, to have our hands filled with Him, and then come to the place which He has appointed, to the very ground of unity, to enjoy this rich and glorious Christ with God's children and with God Himself.

Chapter Sixteen

THE ISSUE OF THE LAND—
THE TEMPLE AND THE CITY

Scripture Reading: Deut. 12:5-7, 17-18; 8:7-9; Eph. 1:22-23;
2:19-22

We have seen much concerning the experience of Christ.
We have begun with the lamb of the passover and passed
through many different items such as the daily manna, the
cleft rock with the flowing stream, the Ark of the Testimony
with its enlargement, the tabernacle, all the various offerings,
the priests with the priesthood, and the holy army. Eventually we have come to the land, the all-inclusive land. We have
seen that this land is everything both to God and to the
people of God. The picture is abundantly clear.

THE INCREASING SCALE OF OUR EXPERIENCE

All the items from the lamb to the land are types of Christ.
Each one, as a type, is complete and perfect in itself, but the
last one, the land, is the all-inclusive and greatest type. The
passover lamb as a type of Christ is indeed complete and perfect, yet it is a type of Christ on a much smaller scale. As far
as the Lord Himself is concerned, He is not circumscribed, but
as far as our experience of Him is concerned, there is such a
limitation. When we come to the Lord and accept Him as our
Redeemer, the Christ we receive is whole, complete, and perfect, but as far as our experience of Him is concerned, we
experience Him only on a small scale, just as a little lamb.

From the time we experienced Christ as the lamb, we have
always been progressing and advancing; we have continually
made improvement in our experience of Christ and have
enjoyed Him more and more. This does not mean that Christ

has become larger and larger. No, Christ is the same, but according to our experience we sense that He is greater and greater to us. Day by day in our experience, Christ is becoming greater and greater. At the stage of our experience in which we reach the last item, the all-inclusive land, Christ is unlimitedly great to us. He is a spacious land. He is a land whose dimensions are the breadth, the length, the depth, and the height. There is no limit to the breadth and the length; there is no limit to the depth and the height. No one can tell you how great Christ is—His spaciousness is unlimited. This is the land we have entered. The other items can be measured. There is an extent, a limit, to the features and experiences of the Christ they prefigure. Not so with the land. The Christ who is typified by the land is inexhaustible and immeasurable.

MATURITY AND WORK

When we enjoy Christ as the lamb, God demands that we stop all our work. At the time of the passover, no one was allowed to work—all work must be stopped (Exo. 12:16). There was nothing to do but enjoy the lamb. The blood was put upon the door, and the meat of the lamb was eaten within the house. There was nothing more to do. The same applied to the eating of the manna. The manna came down from heaven for their enjoyment. Nothing needed to be done but simply to take and enjoy it. So it is when we enjoy Christ in such a way. When we take Him as our Savior and as our daily food supply, there is absolutely nothing for us to perform. We only need to accept freely and fully what has already been provided. Any manner of work from us can only hinder the enjoyment of Christ in these aspects and would be an insult to God.

But when we come to the Ark, it is a different story: there remains something for us to do. With the experience of Christ as the Ark we have the building up of the tabernacle. The aspect of work is even further intensified when we come to the land, for as we have already seen, unless we work upon the land, it will produce nothing for us. The land is indeed different from the lamb and the manna. The manna descended with the dew from heaven (Num. 11:9). There was no work required for its enjoyment but simply to rise, gather, and partake. But when the people of Israel entered the land and began to enjoy its goodness, the manna from heaven ceased, and the fruit of the land took its place as their food supply (Josh. 5:12). We must be deeply impressed with this difference: to enjoy the manna requires no work, but to enjoy the produce of the good land depends very much upon our work. It is entirely different.

When we are newly saved and spiritually immature, we do enjoy Christ. He is so good and wonderful to us! Oh, Christ is our lamb, our daily manna, and our rock with the flowing stream—He is so good! He does everything for us! But as we gradually mature in the Lord, we discover that we have something to do. We must bear some responsibility; we must work. In our human families, for instance, there are the little ones, the infants and the toddlers. They have nothing to do but enjoy what is being continually provided for them. Everything for them is prepared by others. But when they grow a few more years, they are given a little responsibility in the family, perhaps looking after some younger members, perhaps doing some minor chores. Then when they mature a few more years, they are charged with greater responsibility. And when they reach the age of twenty or more, they must take employment and earn their entire living. It is exactly the same in the spiritual realm. When we enter into the all-inclusiveness of Christ, we enjoy much more of Him. But at the same time there is considerable responsibility which must be taken by us. The more we work on Christ, the more we will produce of Christ, the more we will enjoy Christ, the more we will have of Christ to share with others, and the more we can offer Christ to God. All this depends on the amount of our labor upon Christ. When we enter the land, we must work!

Brothers and sisters, when are you going to have your corporation registered in your city? What corporation? Christ Incorporated! Christ Incorporated, Los Angeles! Christ Incorporated, San Francisco! Christ Incorporated, Sacramento! Every group of believers as a local expression of the Body of Christ must be a corporation, a factory to turn out Christ in mass production. We must be working on Christ and producing Christ day by day. We must make Christ our industry. If others ask us what our business is, we should be able to answer that it is Christ, and our firm is Christ Incorporated. We want to see that this corporation will have branches in every city throughout the entire world. How wonderful if everywhere we go there would be this reality—a group of people whose only business is Christ. Christ Incorporated, London! Christ Incorporated, Paris! Christ Incorporated, Tokyo! Sometime we can have a world fair. Christ Incorporated in Taipei can bring something. Christ Incorporated in Hong Kong can bring something. From every city the Lord's children can bring the Christ they have produced and have an exhibit of His manifold riches. Let us come together to have an exhibition of Christ. We are not speaking of some kind of human organization but of those who are built together in Christ in a practical way, whose only purpose is to work upon Him in order to produce Him, enjoy Him, share Him, and express Him. This is what God intends that we do.

Consider again the people of Israel in the ancient times. After one year of laboring upon the good land, cultivating the ground, sowing the seed, watering and pruning the plants, the day of the Feast of Tabernacles came. Then from all over the land, from all the cities and towns, the people came together to their center in Jerusalem, bringing the tithes and firstfruits of their produce. There was an exhibition of all the products of the land of Canaan. This feast together with God's people and with God Himself all depended upon their diligent work on the land.

Now we are enjoying Christ as the very reality of that exceeding good land. It is indeed the grace of God to give us such a land, but it is a matter which involves our full cooperation. We must cooperate and coordinate with God. God has prepared and provided this piece of land—that is, God has given us Christ. And God has poured out the rain from heaven upon this land—that is, God has given us the Holy Spirit. The land is the type of Christ, and the rain is the type of the Holy Spirit. Yet there is the need of our cooperation. We must cooperate with God; then we will have the produce. How much do we cooperate with God? This is the problem.

In some so-called churches, you cannot realize that anything exists as the produce of the good land. All they can afford people is the lamb of the passover and the manna from heaven. All they can minister to people is Christ as the redeeming lamb or Christ as the daily manna. They cannot minister Christ as the good land because they themselves have never entered the good land. But in some local churches, when you contact the people and attend their meetings, you realize that whenever they come together, there is a rich exhibition; all kinds of the produce of Christ are displayed. Why? Because they have entered the good land and they are working diligently upon Christ. They have many good things which they have produced from Christ.

THE PEACE OFFERING

We must notice again that all the people of Israel brought their produce to one place, to the place chosen by God, to worship God and to enjoy the produce before God and with God. What they produced, typically speaking, was Christ, and what they offered to God was Christ. What they produced they offered to God to enjoy mutually before Him and with Him.

One of the offerings which God's ancient children offered was rather distinct and special. It was the peace offering. In the peace offering there was something for the one who offered it to enjoy, there was something in it for others to enjoy, and there was also something for God to enjoy. If I came to offer the peace offering, there would be a part for me, a part for others, and a part for God. Read Leviticus, chapter 7. You will see that the peace offering is an offering to be enjoyed by the one who offers it and to be shared with others and with God.

Brothers and sisters, every time we come together to worship God in Christ, with Christ, and through Christ, we are offering Christ as the peace offering. And with this Christ, there is a part for God, a part for us, and a part for others. We enjoy Christ mutually with God and before God. This is the real worship, and this is the heaping of shame upon the enemy, Satan.

THE TEMPLE

We must be deeply impressed with the word in Deuteronomy 12—it is extremely important. We must bring all our produce to the place chosen by God. What is this place? It is the place of God's habitation. You must bring Christ to this central point; I must bring Christ to this central point; we all must bring Christ to this central place, there to mutually enjoy Him before God and with God. This will result in the habitation of God. We must realize that when we enjoy Christ not only in an individual way but in a corporate way, there will be an issue. The habitation of God will come into being. That means that on this earth, in this age, at this very moment, God will have a place to dwell. Brothers and sisters, when we enjoy Christ to a certain extent and when we come together to enjoy Christ before God and with God, this fact emerges—we are the habitation of God; God dwells among us. When anyone asks where God is, we may tell them to come and see. If we want to find a brother or a sister, we go to their home, their habitation. There we will see them; there we can commune with them. People today are asking where God is. They are saying, "You preach God, but where is God?" If we are those who enjoy Christ as the good land to such an extent that we come together upon the ground of unity to enjoy Him mutually with God, we will be the proper church. If we have such a situation and people ask us where God is, we can answer, "Come and see. God is in His home. Now God has obtained a dwelling place upon this earth."

Let me illustrate. If you come to a city and wander throughout it day by day, having no certain dwelling place, it will be extremely difficult to locate you. A letter addressed to you could hardly be delivered by the post office. But if you settle down in a particular house on a certain street in a certain district, you will have a definite address. Anyone can locate you.

You and I who are believers are talking continually about God. But the unbelievers are asking, "Where is God? You talk so much about Him, but where is He?" You may answer that God is so great; God is omnipresent; God is everywhere. But I wish to tell you that when we enjoy Christ in a corporate way to a certain extent, God, in a certain and real sense, will be localized. He will have a definite address on this earth. You can say to your friends, "Come and see God. Come to the habitation of God. Come to His home." The home of God is the very place where "Christ Incorporated" is. Wherever you go, if you can find "Christ Incorporated," there is the home of God. Chapter 14 of 1 Corinthians tells us that when Christians come together in the proper way, people will come in and bow down, acknowledging that God is truly among them. In other words, they will confess that it is the habitation of God.

Of what is this habitation, this home of God, built? It is built of Christ mingled and blended with so many believers. With them, Christ is everything. He is the all-inclusive land to them. Christ is what they eat, Christ is what they drink— Christ is everything to them.

Take a healthy, American youth for example. Every cell in his body is American. He was born in America, he was brought up in America, and he is saturated and constituted with the produce of America. All his living has been reaped from the land of America. He has eaten American eggs, American beef and chicken, American potatoes, oranges, and apples, etc. Day by day he has been eating America, and day by day America has been digested by him and mingled with him. He has become a part of America. He is one hundred percent American.

In exactly the same principle, a Christian is a Christ-man. A Christian is one who day by day is eating Christ, drinking Christ, digesting Christ, becoming mingled with Christ. After some time, Christ to a certain extent becomes this man. If you are an American, you need not tell others. Most anywhere you go in the world, people will recognize you as such. There are certain distinguishing characteristics that mark you out as an American, one of which is the things you eat. In like manner, if you are Chinese, everyone knows it. If you know what the Chinese people eat, you only need to exercise your sense of smell to discern their origin and constitution. It is rather difficult sometimes to distinguish the Japanese from the Chinese. Just by looking at their eyes, it cannot be easily discerned. But if you are familiar with the diet of both the Chinese and the Japanese, you may distinguish them by using your sense of smell. The Japanese eat certain foods which emit certain odors, and the Chinese eat different foods which emit different odors. In other words, you become what you eat, and you are known by what you eat. Just as an American is something of America, so a Christian is something of Christ. This morning he eats a little of Christ, and this evening he eats a little of Christ. Day by day he eats Christ and drinks Christ. Christ is gradually digested by him and mingled with him so that he and Christ become one. Then when he comes together with other Christians who have done the same thing, he brings Christ and they too bring Christ. Christ is everything to them. Christ is their very constitution. Wherever they go, they cannot help but bring Christ. When they meet together, they offer Christ to God, they enjoy Christ together, and they exhibit Christ. Whenever they speak, Christ comes out. Everything is Christ. This is the habitation of God; this is the home of God.

It is abundantly clear that this is the real church, the real expression of the Body of Christ. It is a group of people mingled with Christ, saturated with Christ, enjoying Christ day by day, and coming together with nothing but Christ. They enjoy Christ mutually, and they enjoy Christ before God and with God; therefore, God is among them. At that very moment they are the habitation of God; they are His house, His home. The habitation of God is the temple of God. And if we have the temple of God, we have the presence of God and the service of God.

THE CITY

But this temple of God needs enlargement. How can it be enlarged? It is enlarged by Christ as the authority of God. We not only need Christ as our enjoyment but Christ as the authority of God. This is exceedingly real. When you and I enjoy Christ together in the way that we have shown, the reality of the authority of Christ is among us. In such an enjoyment and out of such an enjoyment, we will be very submissive to God and to one another. We will be full of submission. Can you believe that after enjoying Christ in such a way we could quarrel with each other? Can you believe that in such an enjoyment we could hate one another? It is impossible. Is it possible for us to be formed as an army to fight the enemy and yet within the army to be fighting with each other? It is possible if this is not an army. If we are a group of bandits or gangsters, it is possible. Without submission there is no army. When we enjoy Christ to such an extent, every one of us will be submissive to each other. We cannot do otherwise. True love is in submission. When we submit one to another, we are really loving one another. True love does not exist in my taste, my choice, or my desire but in my submission. If there is submission among us, the authority of Christ is among us. It is the authority of Christ that enlarges the habitation of God, the temple of God.

What is the enlargement of the temple of God? It is the city of God. By the authority of Christ, the church is not only God's home but also His city. Not only is the presence of God there but also the kingdom of God and the authority of God. When people come in, they will sense God's presence, and they will also sense God's authority. They will say that this is not only the house of God but the kingdom of God. Then there will be the city with the temple. The city and the temple are where there is a group of people who experience and enjoy Christ to such an extent that they are mingled and blended with Him in every way. When they come together, they enjoy Christ before God and with God. Everything with them is Christ. If we are in such a situation, praise the Lord, we have the house of God and we have the city of God. We are in God's home, and we are in God's kingdom. All who come into our midst will sense the presence of God as well as the authority of God. They will say, "God is not only dwelling here, but God is ruling here."

Brothers and sisters, this is what God is seeking today. He is looking for such a situation on this earth, in the very place where you are living. If you are living in Louisville, God is seeking this in Louisville. If you are living in Sacramento,

God is seeking this very reality in Sacramento. Wherever we are living, God is seeking His house and His kingdom, His temple and His city, among us. But we must experience Christ. Starting with the passover lamb and passing through so many experiences, we must come together with the saints into the land, the all-inclusive Christ. Then we must labor diligently upon the land to produce the abundant riches of Christ. We must become "Christ Incorporated," the group of Christians who produce Christ, enjoy Christ, share Christ, and offer Christ to God in worship. Everything with us must be Christ. This is the real expression of the Body of Christ. Here is the house of God and the kingdom of God. If we have such a reality, we have the land, we have the temple, and we have the city.

We cannot now go into detail concerning the temple and the city. But at the present we do know something about the land—how to get into it, how to take possession of it, how to enjoy it and live within it, how to labor upon it, how to worship God in it, and how to have the temple and the city built upon it. We are clear that the land is Christ Himself, and the temple and the city are the fullness of Christ. Christ is the Head, and the fullness of Christ is the Body, the church. In these messages we have been speaking of the land with the temple and the city. This is Christ with the church, His Body, the fullness of Him who fills all in all.

This is what God is seeking today. May we be faithful to Him and learn by His grace how to enjoy Christ, how to experience Christ, and how to apply Christ to our daily lives. Then we will continually grow in our experience and enjoyment of Him until that time when with the saints we enter the good land, labor upon it, and the temple and the city come into being.

ABOUT THE AUTHOR

Witness Lee was born in 1905 in northern China and raised in a Christian family. At age 19 he was fully captured for Christ and immediately consecrated himself to preach the gospel for the rest of his life. Early in his service, he met Watchman Nee, a renowned preacher, teacher, and writer. Witness Lee labored together with Watchman Nee under his direction. In 1934 Watchman Nee entrusted Witness Lee with the responsibility for his publication operation, called the Shanghai Gospel Bookroom.

Prior to the Communist takeover in 1949, Witness Lee was sent by Watchman Nee and his other co-workers to Taiwan to ensure that the things delivered to them by the Lord would not be lost. Watchman Nee instructed Witness Lee to continue the former's publishing operation abroad as the Taiwan Gospel Bookroom, which has been publicly recognized as the publisher of Watchman Nee's works outside China. Witness Lee's work in Taiwan manifested the Lord's abundant blessing. From a mere 350 believers, newly fled from the mainland, the churches in Taiwan grew to 20,000 in five years.

In 1962 Witness Lee felt led of the Lord to come to the United States, settling in California. During his 35 years of service in the U.S., he ministered in weekly meetings and weekend conferences, delivering several thousand spoken messages. Much of his speaking has since been published as over 400 titles. Many of these have been translated into over fourteen languages. He gave his last public conference in February 1997 at the age of 91.

He leaves behind a prolific presentation of the truth in the Bible. His major work, *Life-study of the Bible,* comprises over 25,000 pages of commentary on every book of the Bible from the perspective of the believers' enjoyment and experience of God's divine life in Christ through the Holy Spirit. Witness Lee was the chief editor of a new translation of the New Testament into Chinese called the Recovery Version and directed the translation of the same into English. The Recovery Version also appears in a number of other languages. He provided an extensive body of footnotes, outlines, and spiritual cross references. A radio broadcast of his messages can be heard on Christian radio stations in the United States. In 1965 Witness Lee founded Living Stream Ministry, a non-profit corporation, located in Anaheim, California, which officially presents his and Watchman Nee's ministry.

Witness Lee's ministry emphasizes the experience of Christ as life and the practical oneness of the believers as the Body of Christ. Stressing the importance of attending to both these matters, he led the churches under his care to grow in Christian life and function. He was unbending in his conviction that God's goal is not narrow sectarianism but the Body of Christ. In time, believers began to meet simply as the church in their localities in response to this conviction. In recent years a number of new churches have been raised up in Russia and in many eastern European countries.

OTHER BOOKS PUBLISHED BY
Living Stream Ministry

Titles by Witness Lee:

Abraham—Called by God	0-7363-0359-6
The Experience of Life	0-87083-417-7
The Knowledge of Life	0-87083-419-3
The Tree of Life	0-87083-300-6
The Economy of God	0-87083-415-0
The Divine Economy	0-87083-268-9
God's New Testament Economy	0-87083-199-2
The World Situation and God's Move	0-87083-092-9
Christ vs. Religion	0-87083-010-4
The All-inclusive Christ	0-87083-020-1
Gospel Outlines	0-87083-039-2
Character	0-87083-322-7
The Secret of Experiencing Christ	0-87083-227-1
The Life and Way for the Practice of the Church Life	0-87083-785-0
The Basic Revelation in the Holy Scriptures	0-87083-105-4
The Crucial Revelation of Life in the Scriptures	0-87083-372-3
The Spirit with Our Spirit	0-87083-798-2
Christ as the Reality	0-87083-047-3
The Central Line of the Divine Revelation	0-87083-960-8
The Full Knowledge of the Word of God	0-87083-289-1
Watchman Nee—A Seer of the Divine Revelation ...	0-87083-625-0

Titles by Watchman Nee:

How to Study the Bible	0-7363-0407-X
God's Overcomers	0-7363-0433-9
The New Covenant	0-7363-0088-0
The Spiritual Man 3 volumes	0-7363-0269-7
Authority and Submission	0-7363-0185-2
The Overcoming Life	1-57593-817-0
The Glorious Church	0-87083-745-1
The Prayer Ministry of the Church	0-87083-860-1
The Breaking of the Outer Man and the Release ...	1-57593-955-X
The Mystery of Christ	1-57593-954-1
The God of Abraham, Isaac, and Jacob	0-87083-932-2
The Song of Songs	0-87083-872-5
The Gospel of God 2 volumes	1-57593-953-3
The Normal Christian Church Life	0-87083-027-9
The Character of the Lord's Worker	1-57593-322-5
The Normal Christian Faith	0-87083-748-6
Watchman Nee's Testimony	0-87083-051-1

Available at
Christian bookstores, or contact Living Stream Ministry
2431 W. La Palma Ave. • Anaheim, CA 92801
1-800-549-5164 • www.livingstream.com